JEWELRY
Fundamentals of Metalsmithing

Tim McCreight

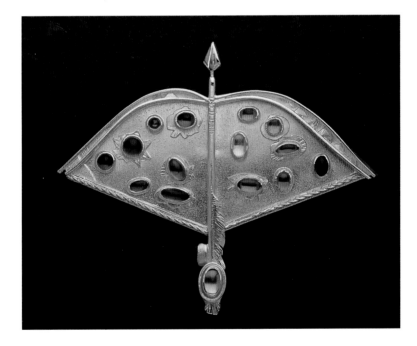

Hand Books Press
MADISON, WISCONSIN

Jewelry: Fundamentals of Metalsmithing
By Tim McCreight

Photographer (studio demonstrations): Robert Diamante
Book Designer: Jane Tenenbaum
Cover Designer: Stephen Bridges
Editor: Katie Kazan
Editorial Assistants: Sarah Mollet, Jennifer Thelen

© 1997 by Hand Books Press

Thanks to *Metalsmith* magazine for providing many of the images shown in this book.

10 9 8 7 6 5 4 3 2

Published by
Hand Books Press, a joint venture of
THE GUILD and Design Books International
931 East Main Street #106 • Madison, WI 53703 USA
TEL 608-256-1990 • TEL 800-969-1556 • FAX 608-256-1938
guild@guild.com • http://www.guild.com

U.S. Distribution
North Light Books, an imprint of F&W Publications, Inc.
1507 Dana Avenue • Cincinnati, OH 45207
TEL 513-531-2222 • TEL 800-289-0963

Overseas Distribution
Design Books International
5562 Golf Pointe Drive • Sarasota, FL 34243
TEL 941-355-7150 • FAX 941-351-7406

Printed in Hong Kong

ISBN 1-880140-29-2

Front cover artwork: (top) Jan Baum, *Structure* pendant/locket, photo by Phil Harris; (center, left to right) Merideth Young, fibula; Nancy E. Fleming, *Waiting for Guinevere* brooch; Pauline Warg, wedding rings; (bottom) Aaron Macsai, *Panels of Movement* bracelet.

Title page artwork: Stephani Briggs, *Pathfinder* pin/pendant.

Facing page: Susan Kingsley, *Zigzag* three brooches.

Back cover artwork: (top) Anastacia Pesce, *Decision* locket; (center) Jung-Hoo Kim, *The Connection 1* brooch; (bottom) Micki Lippe, earrings.

JEWELRY

Fundamentals of Metalsmithing

Contents

Introduction   6
Author's Note   7

1 CUTTING & BENDING   8

Measurement   8
Layout   9
Sawing   10
Drilling   12
Filing   13
Wire Work   15
Forming   16
Annealing   18

2 PATTERN, TEXTURE & CONTOUR   20

Hammering   20
Roll Printing   21
Stamping   24
Chasing   25
Repoussé   26
Heat Textures   28
Reticulation   29
Mixed Metals   30

3 FUSING & SOLDERING   32

Fusing   32
Soldering   33

Tim McCreight, fibula. 18K. 2½ x ¾". *Photo by Robert Diamante.*

4 COLD JOINING   42

Staples and Tabs   43
Rivets   43
Threaded Connections   50
Adhesives   51

5 FINISHING & PATINAS   52

Abrasive Media   53
Burnishing Media   56
Machine Finishing   57
Patinas   62

6 STONE SETTING 68

Gemstones   68
Basic Bezels   70
Prong Settings   78

7 MECHANISMS & CHAINS 84

Pin Findings   84
Pendants   86
Chains   90
Hinges   97

8 CASTING 102

Direct Casting Methods   102
Lost Wax Casting   106

APPENDICES 117

What Do You Need to Know About Metal?   119
Health & Safety   122
Pouring an Ingot   125
Tool Making: Hardening & Tempering Steel   127
Tool List   129
Tables & Charts   130
   Temperature Comparisons   130
   Alloys   131
   Weight Comparisons for Sheet & Wire   132
   Relative Sizes & Weights   133
Glossary   134
Suppliers   137
Suggested Reading   139

Index   140
Acknowledgments   143

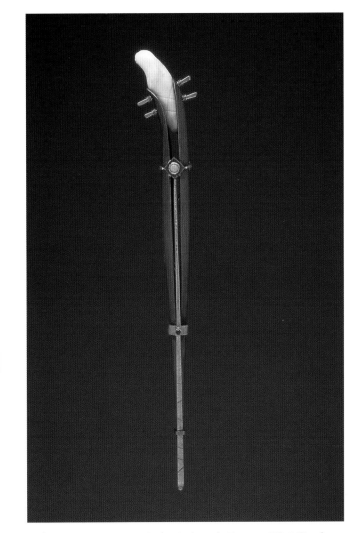

Andrew Cooperman, *Lucy Series #1* brooch. Bronze, 18K, 14K, ruby, opal, tooth, 6" tall.

Introduction

Each of us comes to craft work in a different way. Some approach it as a business, and for others it is mostly a personal—sometimes introspective—activity. For all of us, it is to some degree a form of therapy, a chance to stare the world in the eye and say, "I made this." Whether we're holding a masterpiece or a crude first attempt, the value lies less in the object than in the fact that we made it. Because this showdown with the universe can be a bit scary, it's useful to equip yourself with some information that will make the creative work a little less chancy and the results more resolved. That is the reason for a book like this.

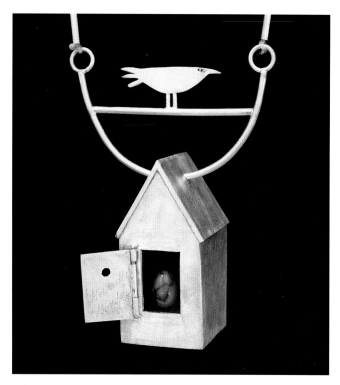

Gabrielle Gould, *Waiting #1* neckpiece. Sterling, turquoise egg. 1 x 2".

These pages contain nothing magical. In them you'll find procedures and tools invented by ordinary people over the last thousand years. Given enough time, you might have invented them yourself, but in the interest of efficiency I've collected the tricks and techniques I consider most useful, and arranged them in a logical sequence.

Jewelry making is fun to teach because the techniques exist as more or less separate components. This means you can make a finished piece using only one or two procedures—simple, but infused with your unique vision. With time, you can acquire more skills and increase your versatility. The processes covered here are "fundamental" in that they provide a solid foundation for further instruction and experimentation, and while this book is written for beginners, it contains techniques intermediate jewelers will find challenging.

What distinguishes this book from others is the huge collection of photographs, most taken just for this use. You'll find clear, grab-it-in-a-glance illustrations that will move you from reader to worker in minutes. The work of scores of talented jewelers fills the book from cover to cover, offering a fresh jolt of inspiration with every rereading.

I've tried to present information in a logical order, but when all is said and done, technique, science and design merge and cross reference, so feel free to jump in anywhere and revisit sections every once in a while. Some details that are elusive at first will be helpful once you've had some time at the bench.

I didn't learn to make jewelry so I could write a book, or even so I could teach it, though I've been teaching metalwork for 25 years. My work at the bench is my response to a universe that says, "Who are you?" I hope you can find the same kind of discovery and fulfillment that the craft has provided for me.

Author's Note

Perhaps the two most important tools you can bring with you as you undertake jewelry making are common sense and creativity. Think of these qualities as favorite pets. Feed them well, give them a chance to exercise daily, and honor their needs. Common sense will help you through the places where a book like this is necessarily brief. It's just plain impossible to describe every step in every process, and while I've tried to be thorough, I bet there will come a time when you scratch your head and say, "How did he get from this step to that one?" I wish I could be over your shoulder to answer, but since I can't, my advice is to use your common sense. How do you *think* I'd get from this to that? You're probably right.

Creative thinking is the ability to see a connection between elements that are not usually associated. Creativity usually starts by asking the right question, or asking a question in the right way. You might not use the traditional method, but what you discover might work better for you. And how do you think all those traditional methods were invented in the first place?

For some, this book will be best used in conjunction with a class, which you might find offered at a local college, craft school or civic program. The advantage of learning in a group is the breadth of exposure and the opportunity to share questions and discoveries. It is entirely possible, though, to learn by yourself—as I did. The basic tools are pretty cheap, a work space can be small, and you can practice on inexpensive metals like copper and brass. All told, you can start a rewarding hobby or promising career in jewelry making in a corner of your basement for about the cost of a set of tires for your car.

One more bit of common sense: take care of yourself. Jewelry making is not terribly dangerous, but any time you use tools and chemicals, there is the potential for accidents. Wear goggles when using power equipment, and a respirator around dust or vapors. If

Beth Piver, *Substantial Presence (being)* brooch. Mixed metals, paint, photograph. 4 x 2¾ x ½". *Photo by Jerry Anthony.*

you are tired or unfocused, don't use power equipment. If you don't understand how a tool works, seek advice, either through books or from local experts. You do not have the option of ignoring these precautions. It's your health, and you must take responsibility for it.

1

Cutting & Bending

I like to begin teaching jewelry making with cutting and bending, which are fundamental to almost every project you'll undertake. You'll need to start with a little information about the tools, the materials and the techniques—then dig in! As you go along, of course, you'll learn more about each of these areas. Supplement this chapter with the brief section on metals in the appendix.

Now that you've decided to make jewelry and bought this nifty book, should you hock the ranch to pay for your new endeavor? No, that's not necessary. There are several reasons why working in precious metals doesn't cost as much as you might fear.

First of all, jewelry is usually small. Even though you may be working in a precious material, you don't need lots of it. In addition, there are creative ways to combine the really pricey goods (gold) with less costly metals like silver or copper. And because copper and brass have similar working properties to sterling and gold, you can practice your craft on those less expensive materials.

Regarding the studio, again we're fortunate, because our space requirement is slight and we work primarily with small tools. Compare that to the potter's kiln or the woodworker's table saw, and you'll

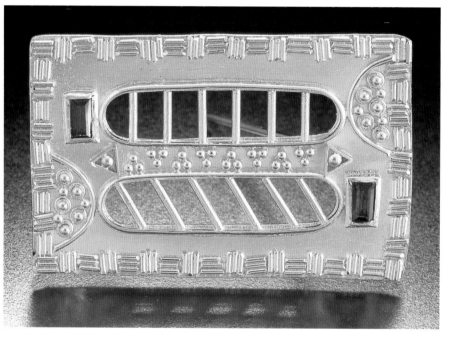

Douglas Harling, *Royal Ghosts* brooch/pendant. 22K, garnets. 1½ x 1".

see how approachable jewelry making is. In the appendix you'll find a list of the tools I consider most important for jewelry making. Write away for catalogs from several of the suppliers you'll find listed there, and use them to sort out your needs. Bear in mind that each jeweler has unique ideas about which tools are most important.

Finally, there is virtually no waste in jewelry making. Almost all scrap, even the dust and floor sweepings, can be sent to a refiner

to be reclaimed. The amount you'll get back depends on the size and condition of your scraps, but as a rule of thumb you can estimate that you'll receive between one-half and three-fourths of the market value back from your precious waste.

Measurement

Most linear measurement in the jewelry world is metric—a system

Joan Parcher, earrings. Sterling, oxidized and gold plated. 3¼ x ⅜".
Photo by James Beards.

Metal thickness, while occasionally described metrically, is more often measured on the *Brown and Sharpe* or B&S gauge. This system, which is used for both sheet and wire, runs from 0 (about the thickness of a pencil) to 36 (finer than a hair). Usually only the even numbers are used, with 10 through 22 being the most common sizes. An-

Donald Friedlich, *Interference Series* brooch. 18K, slate. 2¼ x 1⅞".
Photo by James Beards.

other measuring system you might encounter, especially in the industrial marketplace, is thousandths of an inch, written as a three-digit number such as .040.

Layout

While the term *design* refers to decisions about shape, composition, texture and scale, *layout* means the engineering of parts and relationships. This is the time to calculate thickness, location of holes, and the sequence of operations. Some pieces require great precision in assembly; others are more casual. If a design requires exact measurements, apply the same level of precision to every aspect of the job, from the sharpness of your pencil point to the quality of your ruler. It doesn't work to be "sort of accurate." Precision is an attitude as much as a skill; when it matters, it matters from the very beginning.

Using a B&S gauge to measure the thickness of sheet.

that lends itself to small scale and easy calculations. One of the most useful tools on the jeweler's bench is a small steel ruler showing metric increments. Other useful measuring devices are calipers, either the sliding or the spring version, but to get started a well-sharpened divider, used in conjunction with the ruler, will suffice.

Grady Alexander, *Frog Paradise* pin. Sterling, natural stones. 4 x 3½".

Danielle Berlin, *Little Old Man* brooch. Sterling, bronze. 6 x 2".

Selecting a Saw Blade

	blade size	use with B&S gauge
finest	8/0	26
	6/0	24
	4/0	22
	2/0	22
	0	20
	1	20
	2	16/18
	3	12/14
	4	10
coarsest	5	8

Many people find it helpful to make paper or cardboard models, especially for complicated structures. It's easier and a lot cheaper to do your thinking in paper than in silver, and faster too. File folder stock is a good weight. Useful tools for layout include a steel ruler, a compass, a pair of dividers, and plastic templates for familiar shapes like circles, squares and ovals—but use whichever tools work, from a computer program to a reducing photocopier.

Pencil or ink lines drawn on metal are hard to see, so I use adhesive-backed paper (e.g., Crack 'n Peel) available from office supply companies and print shops. This shows a drawn line clearly and has an added advantage of being erasable like any other paper.

Once your idea is worked out, transfer it onto the adhesive paper, first in pencil, then in ink. Clean the metal with soap and water, or with a Scotch-Brite pad, to remove finger oils. Then peel the backing off the paper and press it onto the metal. Saw right through the paper; when done, peel or burn it off.

Sawing

Sawing is one of the most basic of all jewelry fabrication techniques. You will use it to cut out decorative shapes, to make openings, and to prepare metal for other processes. Because of its simplicity, it offers a directness that allows each worker's gesture to show, not unlike a brush stroke or signature.

SAWING TOOLS

The equipment for sawing is simple, consisting of three elements: *saw frame, bench pin* and blades. A jeweler's saw frame is made of steel with a wooden handle, and is sized according to its *throat*—the reach from the blade to the back of the frame. A typical size for most jewelry work is 3 or 4 inches. This piece of equipment will be with you for years, so avoid skimping. A good frame will cost about $15.

The bench pin is a wooden support on which sawing and filing are done. It is nothing more than a block of wood, firmly anchored to the bench, shaped by each jeweler to suit individual needs. Bench pins can be purchased or made, but either way you'll need to cut away some areas to make the pin ideally suited for your posture and needs. Notice the photograph on page 11; it shows the proper position for sawing, with the hand directly beneath the bench pin.

Saw blades are available in a dizzying array of brands and sizes. Let's make it easy: You get what you pay for. A dozen blades can cost anywhere from 75¢ to $4.00, and with a little experience you will be able to tell the difference. Cheap blades are imperfectly cut, poorly tempered, and inconsistent. Buy at least a mid-range quality to avoid frustration.

Blade Sizes

To cut properly, blades should be matched to the thickness of the materials being cut. The ideal relationship will allow three teeth to touch the metal at any time. The result is a cleaner cut, improved control, and longer blade life. The chart above shows ideal sizes, but you can be off a size in either direction and still saw smoothly.

Sawing goes best when you don't think too much about it. With a simple vertical rhythm, the blade slides through the metal with apparent ease, able to cut out minute details and bold forms. At least that's the idea. It may seem a little jerky at first, but with an hour or two of practice, you will be able to guide the blade where you want it to go. The process of sawing relies on the senses of touch, vision and hearing to find a perfect stroke. This kind of synthesis can only be found through practice.

THE SAWING PROCESS

1 Secure the blade firmly in the frame, teeth pointing toward the handle.
2 Hold the saw frame so the blade is vertical. This grip will feel as if you are reaching under the workbench.
3 Don't grip the handle too strenuously. Be relaxed, let the tool do the work.

4 Track the blade vertically. Don't let it seesaw or stab the metal.
5 Use the entire length of the saw blade, with long, relaxed strokes.
6 Keep the cut moving straight away from you, turning the work—not the saw—as you go.

To insert the blade, rest the front tip of the frame on the edge of the workbench and lean against the handle with your chest just enough to hold the frame in place. With both hands free, pick up a blade and lay it into one of the gripping plates.

In order to cut on the down stroke, the teeth of the saw blade must point toward the handle. To ensure this, look at the blade closely or slide it lightly along a piece of fabric, like your shirt. You'll notice the blade snags in one direction but not in the other—the direction of the snag is the way the teeth are pointing.

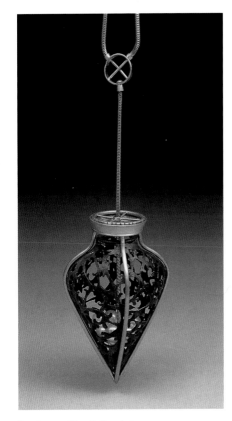

Jan Baum, *Plumb Pearl*. Bronze, copper, cultured pearls. $2^5/_8$ x $1^9/_{16}$ x $1^1/_2$". © 1994.

SAWING

1 Lay out the design on label paper. This design is traced from a photograph.

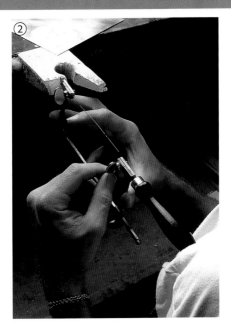

2 Support the saw frame against your chest as you insert the blade.

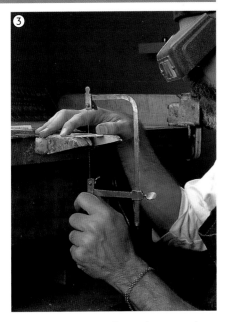

3 The proper posture for sawing: Keep the blade vertical.

(Continued on page 12.)

To make the blade taut, lean against the saw frame as it is supported against the bench. While it is in this slightly "collapsed" state, tighten the free end of the blade in its gripping plate. When you lean back, the frame will flex and the blade will pull tight. When *piercing* (cutting a section from within a piece), the process is identical, except that the blade is inserted through a hole drilled in the sheet before being fixed in the frame.

Drilling

Holes can be made by hammering a pointed tool through a sheet, but a drill bit provides much more control. Bits can be used with any sort of drill, from the traditional bow drill to the simple "egg-beater" style to an electric hand drill or flexible shaft machine. Whatever the tool, start by making a shallow dimple with a center punch where the hole will be. This provides a grip for the drill bit, which tends to twirl sideways unless anchored.

Nicole Danielle Jacquard, *Window Series: Home, Church, Shop*. Sterling, acrylic frame. 4 x 2½" each. *Photo by Kevin Montague.*

Drilling in metal should always be at a slow speed. It is tempting to push the tool into the metal, as if more force will facilitate the penetration, but just the opposite is true. Slow down and give the cutting edges time to shear off thin shavings of metal.

Some people like to lubricate saw blades and drill bits with beeswax or a synthetic alternative. This process is made easy by attaching a lump of wax to the front of the bench near the bench pin, where the tool can be touched against the wax every so often.

SAWING *(continued)*

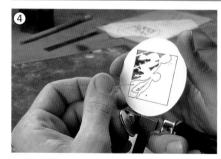

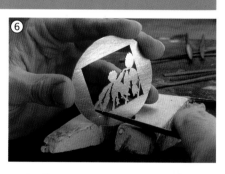

4 Drill a hole in each compartment of the design, and thread the saw blade.

5 Rotate the work as needed while sawing, working in the center of the bench pin.

6 Use small files to refine the shape.

7 The finished pin, with a round wire soldered onto the edge.

Devta Doolan, cuff links. 22K, diamond crystals (loose inside).
Photo by Robert Diamante.

Pauline Warg, wedding rings. 14K rose and green gold.

Heather Croston, *March* pendant. Sterling, paint, wood. 2 x 1¾".

Use a push-and-slide
stroke to file a flat edge.

Filing

As simple as they are, files are among the most important tools in the jeweler's arsenal. They can be used to create forms, refine shapes and alter surfaces. Proper use of files can often make the difference between an acceptable piece and one that is truly special; time spent mastering the use of your files will be repaid many times over.

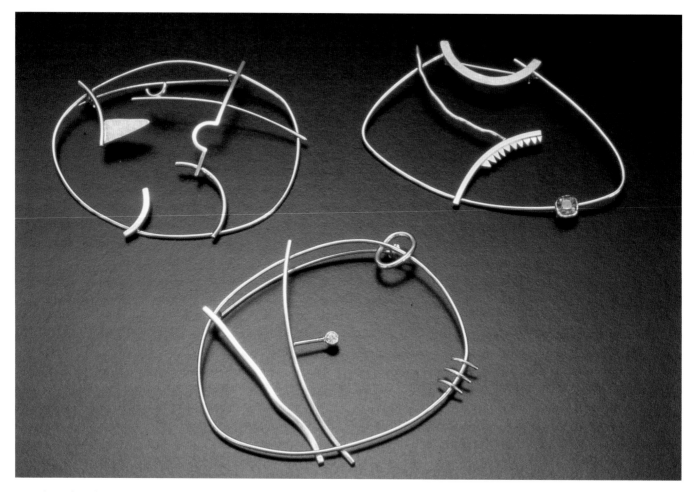

Sam Shaw, three brooches. 14K white and yellow gold, diamond, tourmaline. Shown actual size.

FILES

We all know that files are lengths of steel covered with cutting teeth. But did you know that every aspect of a file reflects a choice, from the quality of the steel to the overall length to the shape of each individual tooth?

American files are described by names, from coarse to fine: Rough, Bastard, Second Cut, Smooth and SuperSmooth. European files are generally considered of better quality, and are available in a wider range of sizes. They are calibrated by numeral, starting with 00 (coarsest) through 0, 1, 2, 3, and so on, up to 8, which is very fine. These numbers are used on files of all sizes and shapes.

On larger files, length is measured along the cutting surface. A 6" file, for instance, has an overall length of about 9", including the *tang*, the pointed section that is inserted into a handle. Just to keep you on your toes, smaller files such as *needle files* or *rifflers* are identified by their overall length, only about half of which is a cutting surface.

Perhaps more important than size is the shape of a file. Use a file that best matches the intended shape, for instance a flat file to make an edge straight and a half-round file when refining curves.

Probably the most frequently used shapes are flat and half round, but square, round and triangular are also very useful, especially in the small sizes. It is impossible to prescribe a single "best" file to own, but these will get your collection started.

Large files should be fitted with handles to protect your palm from injury and to achieve maximum leverage and control. Handles are available wherever files are sold, in both wood and plastic, and can be removed and reused. Be sure the handle has a hole equal to the width of the tang at about mid-length (most come this way), and drive the handle onto the file with

Michael Swanson,
Fish Brooch. Brass.
2 x 3½".

a mallet. Some plastic handles are made to screw onto the tang, and these also work well.

The Filing Process

To get the most from a file, you'll want to develop a proper filing stroke. Be sure the piece being filed is well anchored against the bench; if it drifts away with each stroke, you are not getting the most for your effort. This is a cutting action, so the file must be pushed forcefully against the metal. Put your index finger on the top of the file to press down as you slide it forward, and don't be afraid to put some muscle into the stroke.

The teeth on all files are angled away from the handle, meaning that all cutting is done with a push action. Dragging the file on the backstroke serves only to wear it down, so use a push-and-lift stroke. Start with the largest and coarsest tool needed, then move systematically to finer files as the shape is refined.

Wire Work

Wire is available in several shapes, or cross-sections, all described with the same numerical system used for sheet metal: the Brown and Sharpe gauge. Precious metal is sold in any desired length, priced by weight, while base metals like copper and brass are usually available on spools or in coils. Precious metals are always supplied fully *annealed*—or at their most malleable state—unless specifically requested otherwise. Base metals are usually sold *half-hard*.

DRAWING WIRE

Though you can purchase almost every size and shape of wire, having a *drawplate* makes it possible to buy only a couple of sizes and create what you need when you need it. A drawplate is expensive, but a serious jeweler will find it a very useful addition to the studio. It is used in conjunction with a heavy-

Draw tongs pull a wire through tapered holes of decreasing size in a drawplate.

duty pliers called *draw tongs* that have a coarse jaw and curved handle for a strong grip.

A drawplate is a bar of hardened steel with holes of decreasing size. Each hole is shaped like a funnel, having its larger opening at the backside. The plate is used to reduce the size of wire, and it can also alter its shape. Drawplates are made in many shapes; the most common is round.

When using a drawplate, first mount it in a bench vise so the holes being used are close to the vise. File a gradual taper onto the last half inch of a wire and poke it through the largest hole possible. Grasp the wire with the tongs and pull it through the plate. Try to keep the wire perpendicular to the drawplate, and use a smooth, even pull. Move down the line through successively smaller holes until the wire reaches the desired size. It may be necessary to refile the taper or to anneal the wire after going through four or five holes.

BENDING WIRE

Whenever possible, bend wire with your fingers; they are unmatched for dexterity and control. When more leverage is necessary, choose a pair of pliers with smooth jaws that match the desired bend. Pliers are available in a wide price range, and generally you get what you pay for. Because these tools are an intimate part of the process, avoid the least expensive—they will wear out quickly.

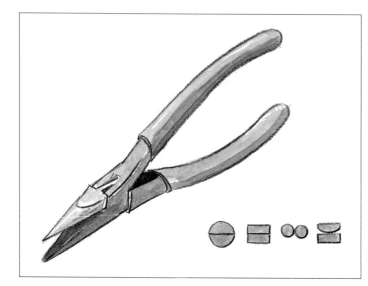

It's worthwhile to invest in good quality pliers. A box joint, like the one shown, is superior to the simpler overlapping joint because of its greater strength. The four most popular jaw styles are shown in the cross section detail: chain, flat, round and ring-forming.

Basic Pliers	
Pliers shapes	**Common uses**
Chain-nose	Most versatile, common bending and gripping
Flat-nose	Opening curves, hardy grip, making square bends
Round-nose	Small curves
Ring-forming	Large curves

Forming

It's typical for a jeweler's early work to be primarily two-dimensional as, for instance, in a flat piece of sheet sawn to an interesting shape. Here are a few basic techniques that push the metal forward, providing depth to make a fully three-dimensional object.

BENDING WIRE

1 File a groove in the bench pin to secure wire for filing.

2 Use round-nose pliers to bend small curves . . .

3 . . . and ring-forming pliers for larger curves.

4 Precision and care are evident in this simple exercise.

j.e. Paterak, earrings. Sterling, pearls.

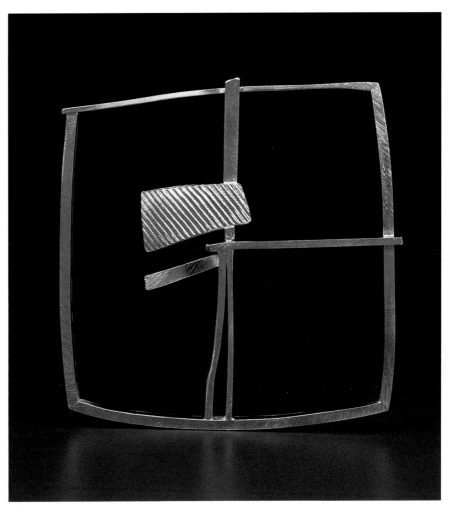

Micki Lippe, *Four Corners* brooch. Sterling, 22K. 3 x 3".

DAPPING

A *dapping block* is a steel cube into which hemispherical cavities of various sizes have been cut. It is used in conjunction with *dapping punches*, steel rods with rounded tips corresponding to the various depressions. Think of a steel mortar and pestle in which the two parts fit together closely.

To use the dapping block, cut a circle from sheet metal and set it into the cavity that is slightly larger than the disk. Set the corresponding punch on the center of the disk and strike it firmly with a hammer or mallet, stopping when the tool makes a thudding sound—probably only a few blows. If more curvature is wanted, move to a smaller cavity, select the corresponding tool, and repeat the process. Continue until you have the desired shape. Domes like this can be soldered together to make beads, or used in a wide variety of other applications.

It's possible to dap metal that has been textured, but this will usually decrease the depth of the marks slightly. Compensate whenever possible by making the texture especially coarse to begin with. When doming a pierced disk, dapping may distort the form.

SCORING

To achieve a crisp right-angled corner, it is necessary to remove some metal, creating a *miter*, as with a wooden frame. This process, called *scoring a groove* or simply *scoring*, can be done on wire or sheet, and

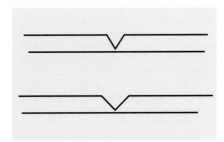

The top drawing shows a groove cut with a triangular file. Follow up with a square file, to create a 90° opening.

is used in making boxes, frames, settings and mechanisms.

When scoring for a right-angled corner, use a square file to make a notch that extends almost all the way through the piece. When properly made, a faint outline of the groove will show through on the back side. At this point the metal can be folded easily. Because this joint is fragile, you'll need to reinforce the corner with solder immediately after bending.

Scoring a strip of sheet metal as, for instance, when making the walls of a box, calls for a special trick. Start by holding the triangular file at a steep angle on the edge of the strip, where it will make a deep, decisive notch. On each succeeding stroke, lower the file slowly until it is parallel to the sheet. By this time there will be a groove deep enough to guide the file and prevent it from slipping side to side. Switch to a square file (or the

corner of a large flat file) to enlarge the groove. To test for readiness, bend the sheet slightly and look at the reverse side. When a crisp line is revealed along the score, the sheet may be bent. With sheet, as with wire, follow this step by soldering the corner to strengthen and protect it.

Annealing

Most jewelry metals have the ability to be rigid or malleable or, as we say in everyday usage, hard or soft. Picture a continuum with maximum malleability on one end and maximum toughness on the other. For some metals, copper for example, this is a long scale—copper can be very malleable or very tough. For others, such as nickel silver, the scale is shorter—there is not a dramatic difference between the two states.

Although every metal has a distinct malleability range, they all have their limits. If you go too far— that is, if you continue to strike or bend or stress a metal after a certain point—it will break. The solution to this situation is the controlled heating process called *annealing*. Precious metals are usually sold in their soft state, a condition called *fully annealed* or *dead soft*. Copper and brass are usually sold half-hard—positioned in the middle of the continuum.

To anneal, set your piece on a clean firebrick or pan of pumice, preferably in a darkened corner of the studio where you can see the heat-colors clearly. Heat gold and silver alloys to 1100°F (600°C), a temperature at which white paste flux turns liquid and clear. This flux is a useful temperature indicator. Copper should be heated to a dull red, and brass until it glows a clearly visible red.

SCORING

1-2 File a notch in preparation for a mitered corner. Bend the corner in your fingers, then reinforce the area by soldering.

3-4 File until the two vertical legs are identical. Set the two pieces together; note that the sides are automatically parallel.

5 The finished frame and a small box made by the same process.

With most precious metals, and with copper, allow the piece to cool until the faint red color of annealing has clearly disappeared. Then promptly quench it in water. White gold and brass should be allowed to cool for an extra minute before quenching. Allowing any metal to air-cool entirely will actually *increase* hardness.

In most cases you will be able to feel the effect of annealing by bending the sheet or wire in your hands. If the metal is too thick for that test, strike a hammer blow and listen to the sound. Annealed metals will give a soft "thunk," rather than a ringing noise.

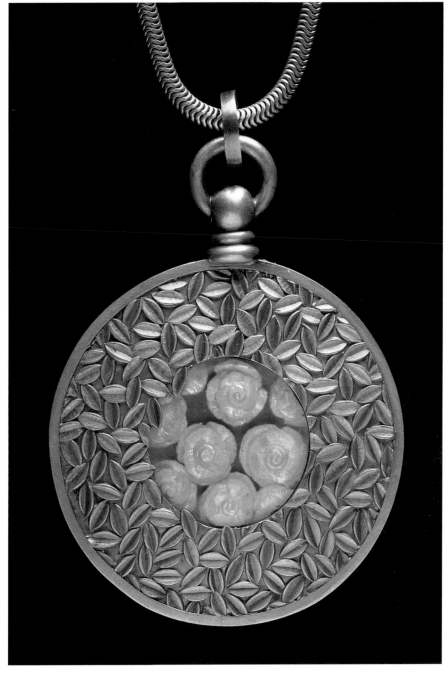

Kate Wagle, *Timepiece: Memento Vita #1*. Sterling, Lucite, paint. 3" diameter.

2

Pattern, Texture & Contour

The real drama of jewelry design comes from altering the metal by giving it pattern, texture and contour. This is vast and vital territory, and will engage your imagination for as long as you make jewelry. In this chapter we'll stick to the basics of surface design. That alone is enough to boggle the mind.

Hammers

The word "smith" (as in metalsmith) comes from the verb "to smite," an old-fashioned term for a strong blow, so it should come as no surprise that hammering is an essential part of metalworking. Hammers come in different sizes and shapes, and can be made of better or lesser steels, but for the purposes of decoration, any hammer that gives the desired mark is the right one for the job.

Even the most tool-challenged person can operate a hammer. Practice on scrap metal to discover the effects of various hammers and to develop a rhythm; then shift to the workpiece. Besides studying the marks made directly by hammers, investigate the wealth of textures you can create by hammering annealed metal against concrete, rusty steel, machine parts, and var-

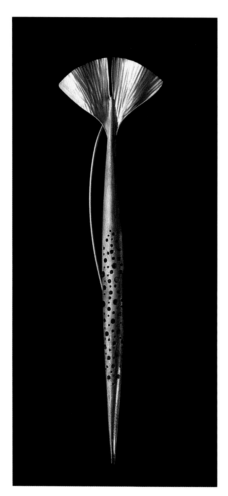

Dawn Eileen Nakanishi, *Zephyr* brooch. Sterling. 5 x 1½".

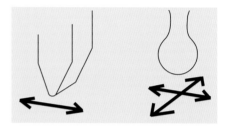

A wedge-shaped cross peen hammer moves the metal in only two directions. A ball peen pushes the metal outward in all directions.

ious textured surfaces. Clean the hammered area with steel wool or Scotch-Brite to see the effect of the marks.

Hammer faces can be carved to create patterns for impact textures as well. Grip a hammer face-up in a bench vise, and work the face with punches, files, saws, drills and chisels. The patterns can, of course, be regular or random, and used alone or in combination.

PLANISHING

The fastest way to alter the shape of metal is to strike it with a hammer. On a large scale, this is called *forging*, a technique used by blacksmiths and silversmiths. A small-scale version used in jewelry making is called *planishing*. Planishing is used to shape metal, at the same time polishing the surface.

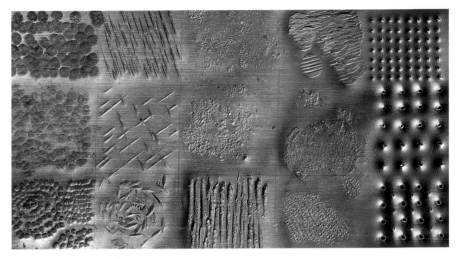

Examples of hammered textures.

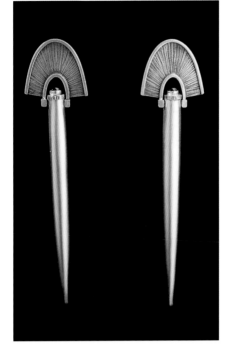

Edie Armstrong, earrings. Sterling, amethyst.

Planishing hammers have a polished face that is slightly crowned (curved). They can be purchased or improvised from any hammer of a convenient weight. Prepare the face by using files, sandpaper and a leather stick as described in Chapter 5. Planish on a heavy piece of steel—a section of railroad track or a heavy stake can be used. This should be mounted at a convenient height on a stable surface.

Roll Printing

This process uses a *rolling mill*, a heavy-duty, bench-mounted tool with two hardened steel cylinders held parallel in a sturdy frame. The gap between the rollers is adjusted to the desired thickness, and the metal is rolled through under great pressure. The usual state of the rollers is mirror-finished, which ensures that sheet metal coming out of the rolling mill is unblemished. The substantial pressure of the mill, which is usually used to thin a sheet, can imprint a texture as well. Follow these guidelines in order to keep the machine in good condition.

Roll Printing Guidelines

- Never force the action.
- Never use wet metal—the rollers will rust.
- Never use steel, titanium, or other tough materials that will scar the rollers.
- When roll printing, always protect the rollers with brass or copper.

THE ROLL PRINTING PROCESS

Anneal a piece of metal to prepare it for taking an impression. This process will work on sterling, gold, aluminum, brass and copper; it is

Examples of planishing.

LEFT: Shana Astrachan, fibula. Sterling. 3" wide.
Photo by Robert Diamante.

BELOW: Peggy Johnson, *Leaf with Interior Heart* brooch. Sterling, fine silver, 18K, 14K, wood. 2¼ x 1⅛".
Photo by Sarah Carson.

not recommended for platinum, white gold, nickel silver or bronze, which are too tough to permit a satisfactory imprint. Any reasonable thickness can be used, but something in the range of 16 to 22 gauge is most common. Thinner material takes a sharper impression.

Textures can be imprinted from fabric, lace, screen, sandpaper, and tough plant materials like bark, woody leaves and dried grasses. Experimentation will be needed and is part of the fun. Cut a sample of the texturing material large enough to cover the metal and set it into place. Cover this with a similar-sized piece of brass to protect the rollers. This sandwich can be fed into the rollers either side up, and should pass through just once, in a smooth, continuous motion.

To determine the correct gap, insert the assembly between the rollers, going just far enough to feel the strain on the handle. The pressure necessary to force the packet through the mill should be considerable, but not Herculean. If you have to stand on the handle to

ROLL PRINTING

1 Use a sharp knife to cut a paper template.

2 Sterling, paper and brass are pulled at great pressure through the mill...

3 ...where the impression of the paper is pressed into the metal.

4 The finished impression.

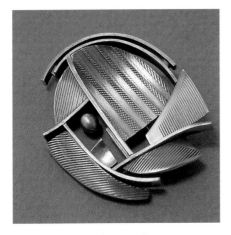

Alan Perry, pin. Sterling, pearl. 2 x 2".

Merideth Young, fibula. Sterling. 2 x 3".

make it move, the gap is too narrow. Retract the packet, open the gap slightly, and try again.

Roll Printing with a Paper Matrix

The effects possible with textures are endless all by themselves, but another way to approach roll printing is to make templates in a desired pattern. Pieces of fabric or paper can be used for this purpose, and will give surprising results. In the example shown, I've used a piece of typing paper, but you should experiment with all kinds of materials.

1 Cut a piece of paper a bit larger than the metal to be printed.

2 Use a razor knife to cut away pieces to make a pattern. Where precision is important, draw the shapes in pencil first.

3 Sandwich the paper between the workpiece and a protective piece of brass. Remember that imprints will be reversed with this process, so double check the orientation of the template. This is particularly important with letter forms.

4 Test the gap in the rolling mill. When it is tight but not impossible to operate, turn the handle in a smooth, continuous motion. You'll notice that the area im-

Metal matrix and tissue ready to be roll printed.

printed by the paper is textured, usually frosted, as if sandblasted. Makes you remember that paper is made of wood, doesn't it? If the original piece was polished to a high shine before printing, areas left by holes in the paper will remain mirror bright.

Roll Printing with a Metal Matrix

In this variation, start by creating a pattern on a tough metal, such as brass, by stamping, hammering,

rolling or piercing. This matrix can be used directly on a workpiece, or in conjunction with paper, which will create a matte texture. For instance, you might pierce a pattern of squares in a brass sheet, cover it with a tissue, and set a piece of sterling on top of that. The impression will have a soft matte texture where the brass pressed against the silver (yes, even with a tissue), but no texture where the pierced holes kept the paper from impact. Metal

ABOVE: Elizabeth Prior, pin. Sterling, 18K. 2 x 2". *Photo by Jon Bonjour.*

LEFT: Kathleen Browne, *Need and Abundance* pin. Sterling, lead, photograph. 5½ x 3¼".

matrices can be used several times, though they will distort a little with each pass through the mill.

Stamping

Like hammering, stamping delivers just what you'd expect—strike a square tool and leave a square mark. It's quick, easy, and nobody gets hurt! Stamps are rods of hardened steel about the size of a short pencil, carved with a specific shape on one end.

Stamp patterns can be as simple as a line or as complicated as a detailed figure, and they can be used in endless combinations. Stamping punches are available through jewelry suppliers. They can also be made in the studio to meet your personal aesthetics; see the section in the appendix on making tools.

The process of stamping could hardly be simpler: Set and strike. Work on a smooth hard surface such as an anvil or surface block, and use a hammer that is heavy enough to do the job, but not so large that it wobbles in your hand. Grip the tool firmly and anchor the heel of your hand on the anvil. Once the tool is in place, direct

your gaze to the top of the tool, and give it a single crisp blow. Avoid tapping it repeatedly—it's likely to skitter around and leave an indistinct mark. If the stamping needs to be in a straight line, you can clamp a strip of wood onto the metal as a guide.

STAMPING WITH SOLDER INLAY

Most stampings are darkened by dipping the work into a patina solution and then polishing the areas

Stamping tools and samples.

in high relief to increase their contrast. Here's another possibility: it's called *solder inlay*.

Clean a piece of copper or brass sheet with Scotch-Brite, then stamp a pattern, taking care that the indentations are deep and crisp. Coat the surface with flux and flood the recesses with hard solder. Be sure that each indentation is completely filled. Pickle the piece and rinse as usual, then file the surface to remove the solder that overflowed the stamped areas. Sand and polish as desired, using a liver of sulfur patina (see Chapter 5). This will darken the base metal and make the solder stand out in contrast.

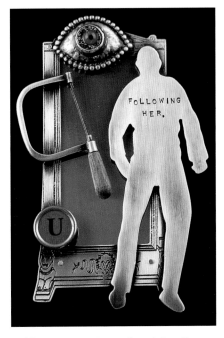

Kathleen Browne, *Accusations: I Saw You Following Her.* Sterling, wood, agate, glass. 4 x 2³/₄".

SOLDER INLAY

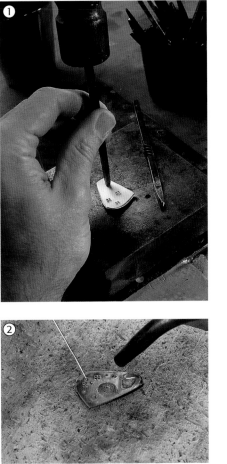

1 Stamp clear-edged marks on a clean sheet of copper.

2 Flood the depressions with solder.

3 File away excess solder. The pattern will be hard to see at this stage.

4 The finished piece.

Chasing

Chasing is an ancient technique in which steel tools very much like stamping punches are used to press down selected areas of metal sheet to create a pattern or image. Historically, this technique was almost universal, appearing in the work of diverse cultures from all around the globe. Though little-used today, there was a time when chasing was considered an essential part of metalsmithing.

Chasing creates pattern and image by pressing some areas down more than others, and some not at all. The process of stamping consists of separate discrete blows: position the tool, strike it, reposition it, strike again. In contrast, chasing employs a continuous tapping motion as the punch is swept across the surface.

Anne Allen, *Patera* brooch. Sterling, fine silver, stainless steel.

Jeff Wise, *Diminutive Infinity* brooch. 18K, opal, tourmaline, pearl. 2½ x 2½".

Some chasing tools have a fine texture on their working surface to create a matte finish. Others are polished and resemble miniature planishing hammers, both in shape and in the shiny marks they make. In chasing, the impressions left by the tools overlap, so the shape of the tool is determined not by the mark being made, but by the shape needed to reach into the contours of the work.

Chasing is traditionally done with a specialized hammer that combines a broad face, a comfortable handle and a springy shaft. In Japan, the traditional tool has a short cylindrical hammerhead and a thin bamboo handle. Any light hammer can be used to get started, but when you consider that a professional chaser might strike hun-

dreds of light blows every hour, it's easy to understand why a comfortable hammer is so important.

THE CHASING PROCESS

1 Draw an outline of the desired form onto an annealed sheet of metal, probably about 18 gauge. Use a steel point to lightly inscribe the line.

2 To more permanently emboss the outline use a *liner*. This tool has a screwdriver-shaped blade, sharpened enough to bite into the metal, but not so much that it might cut through. With the metal well secured, tap the liner lightly as you steer it along the line. Ideally, each blow slightly overlaps the last one.

3 Working on a hard surface such as steel, hardwood or pitch, strike the punch lightly to press down the area around a design. This will make the unhammered area appear raised. The process involves repeated light tapping of the tool as it is guided over the surface, almost the way a pneumatic hammer bounces on pavement during road repair.

Repoussé

This time-honored process takes its name from the French word for "pushed out" and is often seen in conjunction with chasing. In this case, blunt steel tools (you guessed it: *repoussé punches*) are used to give contour to metal sheet before

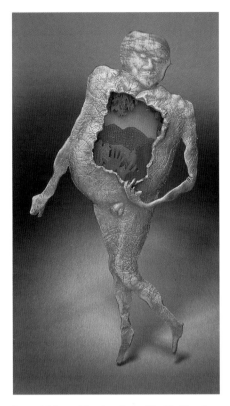

Steve Midgett, *The Jungle Inside My Heart.*
Sterling, titanium, shakudo. 4 x 1½".

Grady Alexander, *Mona Lisa* pin. Sterling.
2¼ x 2".

chasing is used to give detail. Perhaps an analogy from woodworking would help. Imagine a signmaker using chisels to carve away sections of a board to leave letters at the original height. That is like chasing, except that in metalworking we can simply press the material down rather than cut it away. Now imagine that a woodworker starts not with a flat board, but by carving a rounded, bulging form. That would be analogous to repoussé. If the sculptor went on to decorate the curved form with chiseled details, that would be like a mix of chasing and repoussé, a common combination.

Repoussé requires a surface that is soft enough to yield, but hard enough to localize the force of a blow, while at the same time anchoring the workpiece. The mater-ial that achieves this is called *pitch*, a dark-colored resin mixture that is gooey when warmed, but semi-hard at room temperature. Historically, pitch was made in the studio, but nowadays it can be purchased ready-to-use from jewelry tool suppliers. It's worth investing in top-quality pitch, particularly since it lasts a long time. Though the pitch can be used in any container, the vessel made for the job is a thick-walled hemispherical steel pot. Its weight keeps it from sliding around, and when set into a ring-shaped holder made of leather, rubber or rope, a pitch pot can be rotated to any convenient angle.

THE REPOUSSÉ PROCESS

1 Anneal a piece of metal that is at least 10 percent larger than the intended result. This will accommodate the material taken up in height.
2 Use a soft torch flame to warm the surface of a pitch-filled pot and press the metal into position, giving it a slight twist to ensure that no air pockets are trapped under the sheet.
3 Draw the intended image onto the sheet with a pencil or pen, then emboss it with a liner, as described above. This will make the line permanent, and starts the bulging-out process.
4 To release the metal, warm it slightly. Then remove the pitch residue with turpentine. Soften the pitch again with a bushy torch flame and set the metal

Nancy Megan
Corwin,
Epidural
brooch.
Sterling.
3 x 3".

back into it, this time upside-down. The outline will be visible on the back.

5 Use repoussé punches or similar rounded tools to pound the metal into a rounded contour a little higher than the ultimate desired height.

6 Release the work from the pitch (if it hasn't torn loose already) and anneal it, taking time to remove the pitch first with turpentine. Reheat the pitch until the surface is fluid, then set the piece back into place, right-side up. Be sure there are no air pockets beneath raised areas of the piece.

7 Continue to use chasing and repoussé tools to press the metal

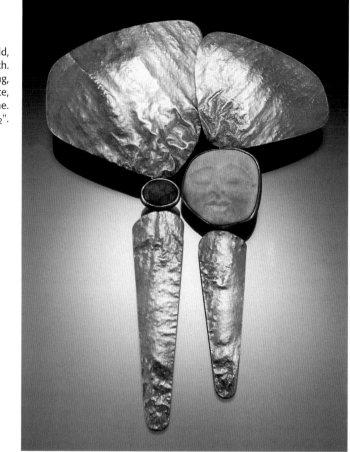

Lorraine Lenskold, *Sedona* brooch. Oxidized sterling, sugelite, carved bone. 3½ x 2½".

Marcia MacDonald, *Shaken ... Not Stirred* neckpiece. Broomstraw, sterling, cast silver spoon, ball bearings (movable), rusted cheese grater, rusted steel. 4 x 2½".
Photo by Richard Gehrke.

down and refine the form. Move the work from back to front to back again, as needed to fully develop the relief. When it is complete, any extra metal can be sawn off and the edges filed smooth. In some cases a flat sheet of metal is soldered on to cover the back.

Heat Textures

Every student of jewelry making learns, to his or her dismay, that when sterling silver gets hot enough, it curls into a boring little blob. This is bad, and in the next chapter we'll look at ways to avoid it. But along the way to that disaster lies an opportunity for some interesting surfaces.

HEAT SCARRING

Heat scarring is a vaguely defined process of using a torch and steel tools to texture metal when it is semifluid. The process is spontaneous, random, unpredictable, and a lot of fun. Unfortunately, it only works on sterling, so you really can't practice on copper and brass as you can with most other techniques. However, you *can* practice with your scraps, and if the results are disappointing, you simply send them to the refiner as you were intending anyway. Nothing ventured, nothing lost.

This process depends on the fact that between being hard and being fluid, sterling silver exists in a "slushy" state where it can be pushed around like putty. Flux the metal and use a large bushy flame, moving it around to ensure even heating, until the surface of the metal starts to shimmer. If the torch is removed at exactly that moment, the skin of the metal will contract, creating an attractive surface of lines and valleys.

You can create heat textures by using the torch alone, but I like to poke at the metal with a steel tool—a piece of coat hanger will work well. At the correct temperature, sterling is soft enough to pick up every mark, responding more like clay than metal. If too much heat is applied, the grooves and textures will melt into a smooth lump, so you'll need to be quick in your actions.

When the texture is right, withdraw the torch immediately. A couple of seconds delay is all it takes to lose a great texture. For some of us, that's part of the excitement!

Variations on Torch Textures

- Sprinkle sterling or gold filings onto a molten surface.
- Drop pieces of *shot* (pre-melted spheres) onto the work.
- Heat pieces over a carved firebrick or a lump of clean steel wool until they slump to create a domed form.

Reticulation

This variation on torch texturing is more controlled and yields a more dramatic texture than the process just described. It depends on the different melting points of fine silver and a copper-silver alloy. The first step is to create a metal with a high-melting "skin." This metal is then heated to a point where the interior collapses.

Reticulation can be done on sterling (92.5 percent silver and 7.5 percent copper), but it is most effective with an alloy containing

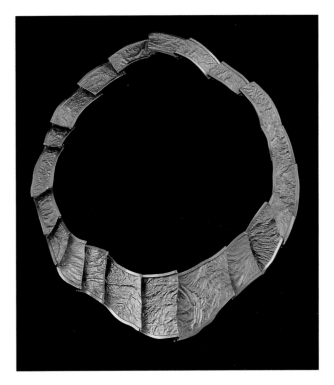

Julie M. Gauthier, *Wave* necklace. Sterling, reticulation silver. 16 x 1 1/4".
Photo by Richard Nicol.

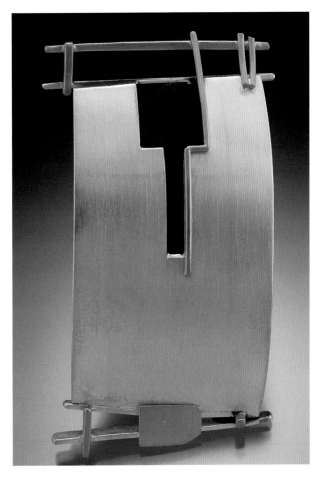

Bruce Anderson, brooch. Sterling, 14K. 2 1/4 x 1 1/4".
Photo by Ralph Gabriner.

more copper. The preferred mix has only 82 percent silver, with the balance being copper. It can be purchased from some suppliers or made in the shop (see "Pouring an Ingot" in the appendix). Either way, the first step is to heat a sheet to its annealing point and quench it in fresh pickle. This will leach the copper oxides from the surface, creating a skin of fine (pure) silver.

Rinse the metal in water and repeat the process at least five times, to thicken the fine silver layer as much as possible.

THE RETICULATION PROCESS

Set the prepared sheet onto a clean fire brick and heat it with a bushy flame held vertically just above the sheet. If the torch has separate fuel and air valves (which is preferred for this technique), add enough air that the flame is almost blown out. Move the torch over the surface to create the texture, noting that the height and angle of the torch will affect the result.

Reticulation is a fairly chancy process, so start with a panel large enough that you can later select the best sections to incorporate into a jewelry piece. Reticulation silver has a lower melting point than sterling, so subsequent assembly should be done with easy and medium solder (see Chapter 3). Because the interior of a reticulated piece is porous, it's best to burnish or press down an exposed edge before soldering it.

Mixed Metals

As evident from the work shown throughout this book, jewelers take full advantage of the rich palette available through metals of contrasting colors. Gold, sterling, fine silver, copper, brass, bronze and nickel silver can all be combined

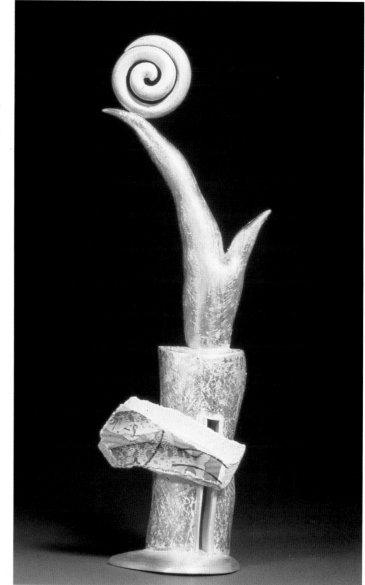

Jung-Hoo Kim, *Some News* brooch. Sterling, 24K foil, used stamp. 4$\frac{1}{2}$ x 1$\frac{1}{2}$".

with traditional soldering. Pieces can be simply cut and placed side by side or on top of each other to create richly colored material. Because most alloys are available in several colors, the range is exceptional.

PUZZLE INLAY

Imagine a very well made jigsaw puzzle in which the pieces snap together with no space between the parts. Now imagine that the parts are cut from metals of contrasting color, and you have the essence of puzzle inlay. Begin by cutting one unit. Refine its shape with files, then trace it with a sharp scribe onto the other piece. Saw carefully, and trim as needed to make the sections fit closely together. Solder as explained in Chapter 3, using hard solder.

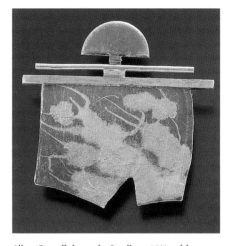

Alice Carroll, brooch. Sterling, 18K solder.
Photo by Tom Mills.

Mary Hughes, brooch. 18K, white and colored diamonds. 4 x 2".

LAMINATION INLAY

This creates an effect similar to puzzle inlay, but is easier. The only disadvantage of lamination inlay is that shapes become distorted, so it won't work for all designs. Start with thick and thin sheets—say,18 and 24 gauge—of contrasting metals. Cut the thinner piece to the desired shape and solder it onto the thicker piece. Run the joined metals through the rolling mill until the two pieces are flush. This can be done in several passes, and the metal can be annealed if needed.

KUM BOO

This traditional Korean process takes advantage of the tendency of pure precious metals to bond together. You'll need a very thin piece of pure (24K) gold, thicker than gold leaf, but still much thinner than tissue paper. Buy the thinnest stock sold, then set it between two sheets of copper and roll it through the mill until the rollers cannot be brought any closer together.

Complete all soldering on a piece made of sterling and pickle it well in a fresh solution. Heat the piece again until it discolors, then quench it in pickle and rinse in water. This process, called *depletion gilding*, leaches copper from the outer layer of the work, leaving a skin of pure silver. Repeat the heat-pickle-rinse cycle at least five times.

After rinsing and drying, set the piece on an electric hot plate. Use small scissors to cut the gold into the desired shape and lay it into position, using a thin film of water to hold it in place if necessary. Wear cotton gloves for the next step to protect your hands from discomfort.

Turn on the hot plate and allow the sterling piece to heat up to around 500°–700°F (260°–370°C), a point where it would be too hot to touch without gloves, but not hot enough to discolor. Press on the gold with a burnisher; if the temperature is correct, the gold will bond. Continue rubbing with a burnisher, and increase pressure slowly as the bond is confirmed. Dip the burnisher in water every couple of minutes to be sure it doesn't get too hot.

Fusing & Soldering

*A*lthough it's possible to make jewelry from single units, it won't be long before you encounter the need to join elements together permanently. The ability to do this with confidence will put you a long way ahead in your jewelry making career. Fusing and soldering are among the most engaging aspects of the field; they both call for a mix of scientific understanding and intuitive response.

Fusing

Imagine two droplets of water on the kitchen counter. If these two beads of fluid come close enough to touch, they will merge together to become a single droplet. That's *fusing.* When a piece of metal approaches its melting point, the outer surface becomes liquid, a phenomenon that enables this basic joining technique.

Jenepher Burton, ring. 18K.
Photo by Robert Diamante.

FUSING

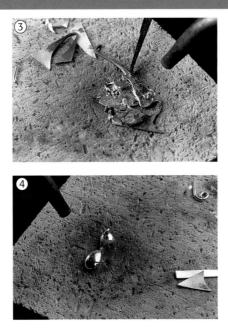

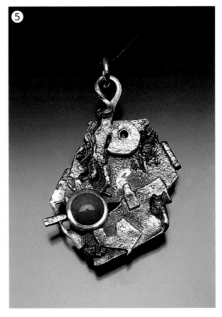

1-2 Set clean, fluxed pieces of sterling on a firebrick. Apply heat so that all pieces reach melting temperature at the same time.

3-4 You can use a steel rod to poke and prod the surface. If you wait too long, the rich textures will roll up into a blob.

5 The finished example.

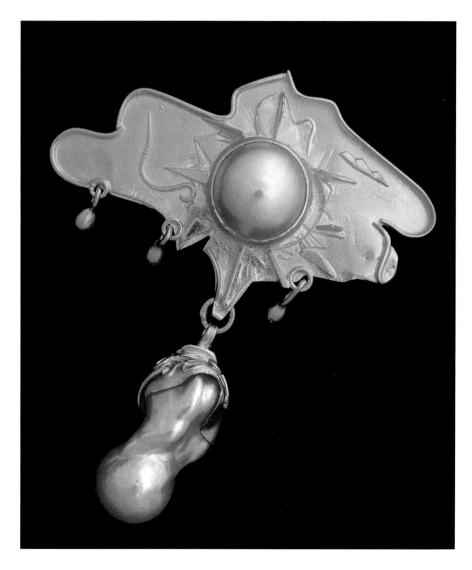

Stephani Briggs, *Cloud Nine* pin/pendant. 22K, 18K, Mabe and blue baroque pearls. 3 x 2½".
Photo by Gary Sheppard.

Some alloys fuse more easily than others, primarily because an oxide skin—if it forms—will prevent joining. And it *will* form, particularly in alloys that contain copper. This explains why pure, nonreactive metals like silver and gold fuse easily, while alloys with only a small amount of copper—such as 22K gold (with 4 percent copper) and sterling (7½ percent copper)—do not. Base metals like copper and brass are at the bottom of the list, almost impossible to fuse except in a controlled environment.

Work on a clean soldering surface, preferably in dim light, so that colors are easily read as the metal starts to melt. Clean and flux the metal, and heat the pieces evenly with a bushy flame; elements must reach the same temperature (color) at the same time. Look for the moment when the surface shimmers like mercury, which is the point where the outer skin of each piece is fluid. Pieces in contact at that moment will be joined.

Fusing is often used in conjunction with heat scarring or reticulation, surface embellishment techniques that can simultaneously weld pieces together. And therein lies the problem of fusing: It risks creating an irregular surface or worse, altering the shapes of elements being joined. If there was no

alternative, I guess we'd get good at fusing and learn to make the best of its accidents. But there is a better alternative.

Soldering

In the case of fusing, increased temperatures break down the bonds between crystals, eventually causing the metal pieces to lose structural integrity. In other words, they melt into formless blobs. This process begins on the surface, which swims in a flash of molten

metal. But just before that point, what happens?

As precious metals approach their melting point, the grains (clusters of crystals) of which they are made pull apart and create microscopic spaces within the structure. Soldering (more correctly called *silver brazing*) is the process of introducing an alloy (solder) that is fluid at precisely this temperature. Because the solder is fluid, capillary action draws it into these spaces in the same way water is drawn into a sponge. Because it is bonded with the parent metal at

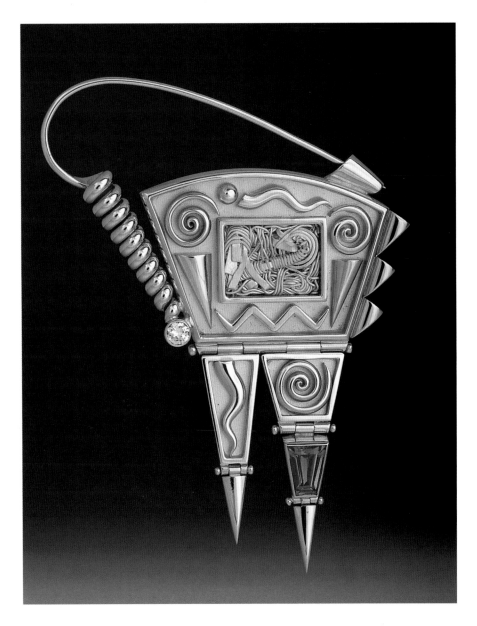

Aaron Macsai, *Spring Bar Pin*.
18K, 14K, diamond, tanzanite.
2½ x 2½".

Soldering Guidelines

1 Pieces to be joined must be clean and must make a good fit.
2 Use flux.
3 Heat the area around the joint to direct the flow of heat to the seam.
4 All pieces being soldered should reach temperature simultaneously.
5 Do not overheat the metal or prolong the process. Hit and run.

Pieces to be joined must be clean and must make a good fit. Because solder will not fill a gap, you can't use it to fill in a space between elements. Remember that the solder is entering microscopic voids, not sitting on the surface. (Keep this in mind when you're thinking about how much solder to use—a little goes a long way.)

Cleanliness is critical to a good solder joint. Unseen oxides and finger oils will prevent solder from flowing into the structure. I always scrub elements with Scotch-Brite or clean surfaces with sandpaper just before soldering.

Use flux. Flux is a chemical formulated to prevent the creation of oxides during a heating operation. Very simply, we can think of flux as an air-hungry compound that absorbs oxygen before it has a chance to combine with metals to make an oxide layer (tarnish) that would inhibit soldering. There are many fluxes, each with its own ac-

this internal level, the joint is very hard and almost invisible. For centuries, this is what has held jewelry together.

SOLDERING OVERVIEW

Soldering is as simple as heat and as complicated as physics. On the one hand, get it hot, introduce solder and hey, presto! The job is done. On the other, each assembly is unique and requires delicate adjustments in timing, flame control and observation. It's like driving. In one sense, once you've learned how to operate a car you can pretty much go anywhere. But every moment of driving requires subtle intuitive adjustments to a unique combination of circumstances.

The following guidelines are important to proper soldering, but they are only abbreviated descriptions of the process and its permutations. There is no substitute for practice.

Andrew Phares, *Two Stories* rings. Sterling, copper. *Photo by Tom Brown.*

All pieces should reach temperature simultaneously. To understand the importance of this, remember that solder works by entering the structure of the metal, a situation that is only possible at high temperatures. If a piece is not hot enough, there will be no spaces between the crystals. If one piece in an assembly fails to reach the necessary temperature, the solder will not penetrate that section, and the joint will fail.

In the workshop, temperature is read through color changes. Because these are easiest to see in a dim light, most soldering areas are shielded from bright or changing light. Having your solder bench in front of a window might allow for a pretty view, but the glare of sunlight will make soldering a lot more difficult.

Do not overheat the metal or prolong the process. Solders melt at very specific temperatures. Period. It's an exact science, and one you should learn to trust. Heating the metal to temperatures above the melting point of solder is unneces-

tive range—the temperature window in which it will do its job. Be certain to use a jeweler's flux with a range of 1100° to 1500°F (600° to 800°C).

Jewelry fluxes fall into two broad families: fluoride-based and borax-based. As a general rule, the former (often a white paste) is messy but has a longer active range than the liquid, fluoride-based fluxes. There are many commercial brands, all of them good and each with its supporters. Try a few to determine which you prefer.

Heat the area around the joint to direct the flow of heat to the seam. Heat flows to a cooler zone. If you do what seems obvious and point the torch flame directly at a joint, the heat instantly heads away from where you want it. To outsmart the heat, start by directing the flame *around* the seam. Think of a target of concentric circles in which the bull's eye is the joint you are soldering. Heat the outer ring, per-

haps an inch or two away from the seam, slowly narrowing the target as the metal warms so that when the piece approaches soldering temperature the flame is almost on the joint.

Kiff Slemmons, *Hand Tools* box with 5 rings. Sterling. 1¾ x 3¼ x 1½". *Photo by Rod Slemmons.*

sary and will do damage. If the solder hasn't flowed when the color indicates the correct temperature, something else is wrong. More heat won't fix it.

It's also harmful to extend soldering time. As mentioned, flux is introduced to absorb oxygen before it attacks the alloy, but just like a sponge soaking up a spill, flux has a saturation point. After this is reached, oxygen will rapidly combine with copper to create stains that penetrate and can ruin a piece, while also weakening the joint. Good soldering calls for careful preparation, controlled heating, and a prompt exit. Get in, get the job done and get out.

GRADES OF SOLDER

Because you are heating everything but the joint itself, areas that have been previously soldered risk coming undone when new seams are being joined. The solution to this problem is to use solders of slightly different melting points.

Gold solder is made mostly of gold, and silver solder is mostly silver. In both cases, a small amount of base metal (usually zinc or copper) is added to lower the melting point. As the proportion increases, the melting point is lowered. In a piece with several joints, the first is made with a high-melting solder, the next with a solder that melts about 50°F lower, and the last with the lowest-melting solder. These are called hard, medium, and easy solder, respectively.

In bygone days, metalsmiths made their own solder as they needed it. Today we buy solder from suppliers of precious metals, and can rely on consistent melting temperatures. In the case of gold, there's another option. A tiny piece of gold of a lower karat can be used as solder for higher-karat gold—for example, a bit of standard 14K will

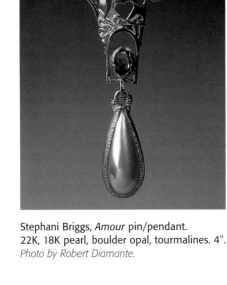

Stephani Briggs, *Amour* pin/pendant.
22K, 18K pearl, boulder opal, tourmalines. 4".
Photo by Robert Diamante.

Popular Jewelry Solder Alloys		
alloy	**flow point**	
SILVER		
Extra Easy	1200ºF	652ºC
Easy	1325	718
Medium	1360	737
Hard	1450	787
IT	1490	809
GOLD *		
10K	1350	732
14K	1375	746
16K	1490	810

* Each refiner sells slightly different alloys that have different melting points. Request a chart when you purchase gold solders.

work as a solder for 18K. Because this lowers the purity of the final piece significantly, it's often preferable to join gold with a solder manufactured for that specific purpose. In other words, you should usually buy 18K solder to work with 18K stock.

THE SOLDERING PROCESS

Solder is sold in sheet and wire, just like precious metals themselves. The alloys are the same for both forms, so melting temperatures and rules apply equally. Why would you chose one shape over the other? Mostly it's a matter of personal choice, and relates to the process of soldering rather than the result. The effect will be the same either way.

Chip Soldering

Sheet solder is used by cutting it into tiny squares or rectangles ("chips") that are set into position straddling a seam. The advantage of this approach is that the solder acts as a temperature indicator: When the metal is at the correct temperature, the solder flows. The disadvantage of chip soldering is that it's time consuming, first in positioning the solder pieces, then in the slow heating necessary to prevent the boiling action of flux from tossing the pieces aside.

Wire Soldering

For these reasons, many jewelers prefer to use wire solder, which can be introduced into the joint at the moment of proper heat. The efficiency of this method is clear, but

CHIP SOLDERING

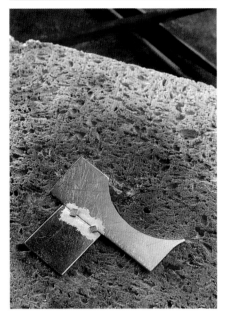

Chips of solder span a fluxed joint.

WIRE SOLDERING

Wire solder touches the joint just as it reaches temperature.

PICK SOLDERING

1 A needle tool is used to pick up tiny spheres of solder.

2 Solder is brought into contact just as the work reaches soldering temperature.

SWEAT SOLDERING

1 In sweat soldering, start by melting solder onto the back of one piece...

2 ...then set that piece onto another. Heat the whole assembly until the solder flows.

because it requires a precise reading of soldering temperatures, it takes a little more experience to master. The trick is to touch the tip of a solder wire to the joint at exactly the moment when the metal is ready to accept it. If the solder is brought in too soon, either the joint won't be made at all, or a blob of solder will fall onto the piece.

Pick Soldering

This useful alternative combines advantages of the first two methods by using pre-sized pieces but avoiding the need to set each chip into place. In this method, sheet solder is cut into tiny pieces that are sprinkled onto the soldering block. A piece of solder is heated with the torch, which will make it draw up into a sphere. It's then picked up with a steel rod like a potter's needle tool or a sharpened piece of coat hanger. The fluxed workpiece is heated to soldering temperature, and the solder is touched to the joint. If the temperature is correct, the solder will jump off the pick to fill the joint. The process is a delicate ballet that requires a little practice, but is very efficient once you get the rhythm. It's especially good for production situations, or multiples like chain links.

Sweat Soldering

Sweat soldering is a two-step process that can be done with any grade of solder, and with either sheet or wire. The smaller unit is fluxed and solder is melted onto its surface. The piece can be allowed to cool down or you can continue directly to the next step. The metal is refluxed, laid into position, and the whole assembly is heated until the solder flows a second time. As shown, sweat solder is very useful for overlay and when attaching findings.

Soldering Aids

It's always best to keep the soldering setup as simple as possible, but sometimes elements need temporary support until the solder flows. Objects in the soldering zone will absorb (or "rob") heat from the workpiece; they're often called "heat sinks". Keep props to a minimum in both size and number, unless your intention is to protect an area from overheating.

Locking Tweezers—These are handy to hold pieces in positions that would otherwise succumb to gravity. The tweezers open when pinched, but spring closed at rest, so you can grip a piece and set it onto the block. Use large bolts or similar pieces of steel to weight the handle end of the tweezers for increased stability.

Third Hand—This device has a heavy steel base and ball-socket coupling that holds a pair of locking tweezers.

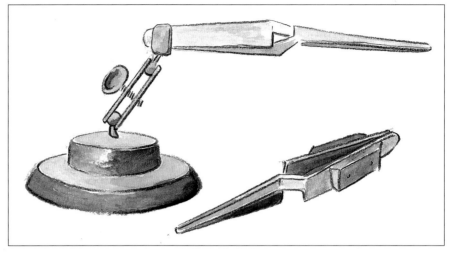

Third hand and cross-lock tweezers. It's sometimes helpful to have pieces clamped into place for soldering. Other tools that can be improvised are paper clips, straight pins and bobby pins.

Susan Silver Brown, *Spirit House Shrine* brooch. Sterling, magnet, copper, 14K, amethyst, brass, paint. 2¼ x 3¼".

Dominque Giordano, necklace & earrings. Sterling, epoxy, gold leaf, pearl. 1¾ x ⅞". *Photo by Ralph Gabriner.*

Binding Wire—Any steel wire can be used to lash pieces together for soldering. Brass or nickel silver wire will work in a pinch, but steel is preferable due to its high melting point. Wrap the pieces loosely and twist the ends of the wire together, then give the wire a half turn with flat-nose pliers to make a "Z." This will tighten the wire, but still allow it to expand during heating.

Soldering Investment—For very complicated assemblies, the pieces can be pressed into wax or glued together, then coated with a plaster-like material called *investment*. Once the investment has hardened and dried, the wax can be pulled away or the glue burned off, and the pieces soldered as usual. After soldering, the investment breaks down when the piece is quenched. It can then be scrubbed off with a toothbrush.

Pickle

Pickle is an acidic solvent that is used after soldering to remove flux residue and oxides. Most studios use a commercial product called Sparex. This is sold as dry granules and mixed with water as needed. As with any strong chemical, mark containers well and keep them safely away from children and pets.

Pickle will do its work at room temperature, but is much faster when warm, ideally about like a hot bath. An easy way to sustain this temperature is with a crock pot, which can be purchased from a housewares supplier. The pot will corrode with use, and must never be used for food again. Before using it in the studio, seal all the seams with bathtub caulking so pickle cannot spill into the interior heating element.

Though less dangerous than strong acids, pickle does irritate

Stephani Briggs, *Sunburst* pin. 22K, 18K South Sea pearls. 4". *Photo by Robert Diamante.*

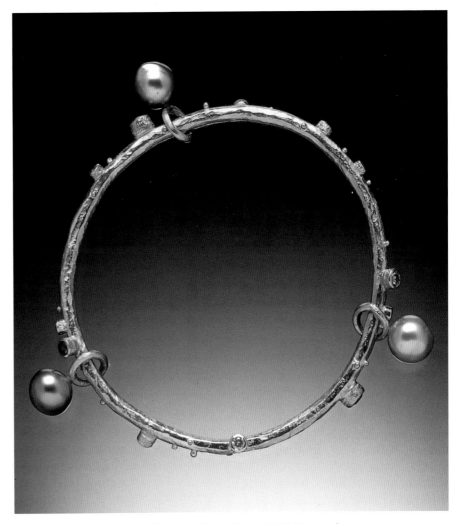

Mary Hughes, bracelet. 18K, white and colored diamonds, Tahitian pearls.

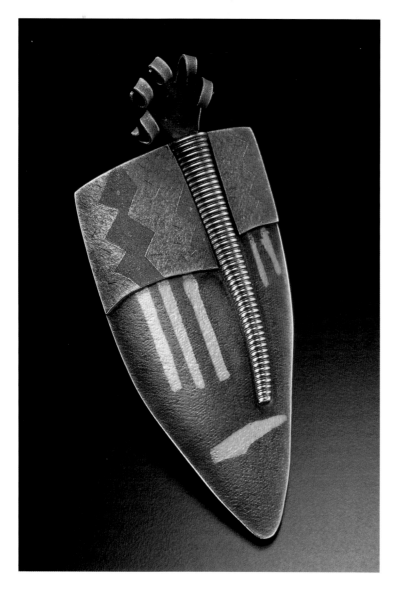

LEFT: Suzanne Taetzsch, *Mourning* brooch. Sterling, 14K. 3½" high. *Photo by Allen Bryan.*

BELOW: Mary Hughes, earrings. 18K, Mabe pearls, diamonds. 2¾ x 1".

skin, especially skin that is cut or chapped. To avoid splashing pickle in your eyes, quench hot metal first in water; that way, if there's a splash it will be messy, but not dangerous. From there, the piece can be dropped into the pickle, which usually takes just a couple of minutes to dissolve oxides. Prolonged exposure to pickle will not hurt sterling or other metals, but it will corrupt soldered joints. For this reason, don't leave a fabricated piece in pickle for longer than a couple of hours.

PICKLE CONTAMINATION

Pickle does its job by leaching out copper oxides, and in most studios, the same pickle is used for sterling, gold, copper and brass. After a couple of uses, pickle becomes a copper plating solution—a saturated acid with excess free copper ions. Those ions are swimming around in there, just itching for a chance to bond with something, and if an electrical charge is introduced, they jump onto every metal surface available.

Because the reaction of steel to acid will create a tiny electrical charge, never reach into the pickle with steel tweezers or introduce a steel wire or attachment into the mix. If you do, anything in the pickle at that moment will become copper plated, the effect being subtle or dramatic depending on the degree of saturation of the pickle. Once the steel object is removed, the pickle is fine again.

This plating action is usually unwanted but there are times when it can be turned to advan-

Solder Troubleshooting

It is often possible to find clues about what went wrong by examining a failed joint.

effect	possible cause
Solder never flowed.	Metal or solder was dirty, oily or tarnished.
	Forgot the flux.
	Not enough heat.
Solder all went to one piece.	That piece was much hotter than the other(s).
Solder balls up.	Solder is tarnished; scrub tarnished sheets and wires with Scotch-Brite before using them again.
Metal has roughened surface.	Too much heat.
Metal has a dark stain.	Too much heat for too long a time.
Joint seemed OK, but later broke.	Heat removed a split second too soon, just as the solder flowed.
	Joint was moved just as the solder was hardening.
	Piece left in the pickle too long.

tage, as, for instance, when coloring brass or gold. Both these metals are difficult to blacken, but copper darkens easily.

To copper plate a piece, wrap it lightly in steel wire (a couple of paper clips will do) and drop it into used pickle. The entire piece will, of course, be plated. However, during polishing the higher surfaces can be returned to their original color, so that copper is left only in the recesses.

Gems and other nonmetals should never go into the pickle. To safely dispose of old pickle, pour it into a bucket set in a sink, and sprinkle in baking soda. This will make a dramatic Captain Chemistry froth, often in a lovely aqua color. When the mix stops bubbling, the acid has been neutralized and the solution can be safely flushed down the drain.

4

Cold Joining

The term "cold joining" means a wide range of devices and techniques that secure two or more pieces together with a mechanical—rather than a heat-induced—connection. Though the term may be unfamiliar, we all use cold connections every day. Paper clips are an example, as are staples, rubber bands, buttons, shoelaces and Velcro. This chapter describes some of the most popular cold connections for metals, but they are merely points of departure. There is nothing here that can't be modified to suit your particular needs. Look around you, not just at jewelry, but at hardware, automobiles, housewares and, well, look at everything!

Despite the thousands of uses for fusing and soldering, there are occasions when the heat of soldering will damage a piece. In these cases, a mechanical (cold) connection is needed. Generally, the reasons to use a non-soldered joint falls into one of these categories.

Use cold connections when:

- The material being connected—stones, plastic, and so on—would be damaged by heat.
- The parts will be easier to polish, patina or set before final assembly.
- The heat of soldering would damage a desired temper.

Jung-Hoo Kim, *Humanbeing-Tree* brooch. Sterling, fossilized ivory, sugelite, 24K foil. 3½ x 2½".

Cleo (Claire Dinsmore), *Autumnal Vestige* neckpiece. Bronze, copper, sterling, steel, 18K, leather, secrets (contents), Colorcore. 3" diameter.

Thomas Mann, *Japanese Stone Fetish*. Steel, stone, brass. 2 x 3³/₄". *Photo by Will Crocker.*

Staples and Tabs

We commonly think of staples as squarish bits of fine wire that pop out of a dispenser we keep in a desk drawer. More broadly, you might consider a staple a simple device that relies on two (or more) legs that penetrate layers of material and are bent over to secure the elements. There is nothing in that definition that limits size, shape, height or complexity. The demonstration photos in this chapter show a simple, fabricated staple, but your imagination should guide you as you explore the wealth of possibilities.

Tabs are a lot like staples, except they usually wrap around a piece rather than pass through it. Because of this, tabs can be sawn to interesting shapes that contribute to the design.

PROCESS FOR STAPLES

1 Lay out the design carefully, paying close attention to mea-surements. If in doubt, experi-ment with a cardboard model.

2 Saw out the pieces and file the edges smooth. Solder elements into place if needed.

3 Bend the legs to 90° to get them ready for the final assembly.

4 Finish the piece as called for by the design, using patinas, pol-ishing, etc.

5 Lay the pieces together and be-gin to press the legs into place. Start by getting everything half-way pressed over to ensure the proper fit. When you are sure everything is in order, press the legs down with a blunt tool or pliers.

Rivets

A rivet is nothing more than a piece of metal—usually a rod or wire—that penetrates all the layers of an assembly and is bulged out on each end to create a head, like the head on a nail. We see rivets in bridges and machinery, and attach-ing handles on our kitchen uten-sils. They also reinforce our blue jeans. Ready-made copper and alu-minum rivets can be purchased from a hardware store, but most jewelers create copper, sterling or gold rivets as needed for a specific project.

Julie Flanigan Hill, *Cuff Link Series: Contains Recycled Materials.*
Sterling, recycled materials. ²⁄₃" diameter.
Photo by Bobby Hansson.

The rivet material should be annealed.
The holding power of a rivet comes from the head, which is formed by tapping directly down on the vertical axis of the rod. This is a process called *upsetting*, and it will be more effective and easier if the metal is as malleable as possible.

Location of the holes is critical. Riveting often comes toward the end of a process, after time has been spent creating, ornamenting and finishing a shape. Don't risk sacrificing that work by rushing through the vital step of locating holes for rivets. When several rivets are being used, as is often the case, avoid

MAKING A STAPLE

1 To solder the legs of the staple, attach an inverted "U," then cut the curved section.

2 Mark the location carefully, then drill holes.

3 Use pliers or a blunt rod to press the legs of the staple over.

4 The finished piece. Sterling elements secure black vinyl (record) to copper base.

Julie Flanigan Hill, *Fortune Series: If You Can Decide What Really Is.* Sterling, rusted tin, rusted steel, lacquered tin, answer from a fortune telling machine. 3½ x 1½".
Photo by Bobby Hansson.

Judith Hoffman, *Bird Goddess* brooch. Sterling, 18K, copper, enamels. 4 x 3¼ x ¾".
Photo by Patrick Sumner.

the temptation to simply hold the units together and start drilling; almost inevitably, pieces shift just enough to ruin the alignment. Instead, use the following process.

Mark, centerpunch and drill all the holes in the top piece. Then set it into position and use a needle or similar tiny point to mark the location of *one* hole in the next lower piece. Separate the pieces, centerpunch the mark, and drill. Repeat the process for each layer. Now, make the first rivet, which will start to lock the pieces together. Note that although they can no longer slide left and right, the pieces can still pivot.

Hold the assembly tightly and mark a second hole, then carefully drill through all layers. Make the second rivet, which will clasp the assembly together so it can neither shift nor rotate. Now it's safe to drill all the remaining holes at once, and complete the riveting.

The rivet must make a tight fit in the hole. Riveting depends on the ability of metal to upset, or compress down onto itself. This only happens when the metal has no other choice, like bending off to the side. To force this situation, the rivet wire must be snugly confined by the hole that contains it. One way to accomplish this is to use drill bits that match conventional wire sizes or are even a touch small. It's easy enough to enlarge a hole with a round needle file.

Another strategy is to drill the holes smaller than the wire you

Jenepher Burton, pins. Sterling, tin and escutcheon nails. 3" diameter.
Photo by Robert Diamante.

have on hand and file a gradual taper in the wire. This wire can be inserted into the hole until it makes a tight grip, and then cut off at the correct length. If the hole is too large, planish the area around the hole in order to push the metal inward.

Provide enough material, but not more. A rivet holds because of its head, the lump that sits on top of the assembly. No head, no rivet. It's clearly possible to cut a rivet too short, but it's also possible to cut it too long. Too much material here will allow the wire to curl rather than mushroom to create a head. If you notice this starting to happen, use pliers to straighten the wire, and file it. The rule of thumb calls for half the diameter of the wire to extend above the surface to become the rivet head. If a rivet wire is 2 millimeters in diameter,

RIVETING

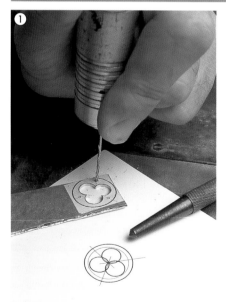

1 Riveting starts with careful layout. Centerpunch and drill holes in the top piece.

2 Use a needle to carefully locate a hole; then centerpunch and drill.

3 Insert a snug-fitting wire and trim it to the proper height.

Steve Midgett,
*Cold Hard Cash,
Hold Cash Hard*.
Steel, sterling,
$10 bill.
1½ x 1¼".

about 1 millimeter should extend from the top and bottom at the beginning of the riveting process.

The top of the rivet should have a flat surface so it will not deflect the hammer blows that give it its shape. If snipping with wire cutters, remember to file the wire's tips enough to remove the pointed ends always left by that tool.

THE RIVETING PROCESS

1 Prepare the pieces following the guidelines above, then slide a piece of annealed wire into the first rivet hole. Snip the wire to the correct length and file it to flatten both ends.

2 Set the assembly on a sturdy steel surface. The tool for this is called a *bench block*, but any handy piece of steel will work; a square hammerhead or a small vise are good substitutes.

3 Hold the work so the tip of the rivet wire on the underside is the only thing touching the bench block. Using a small ball peen or cross peen hammer, strike several light blows against the exposed tip of the rivet.

4 Flip the piece over and repeat the process. It won't take long before the upsetting of the rivet is enough to hold it in place. Continue flipping the piece, working on both sides as the rivet head grows. If using a cross peen hammer, alter the position of the hammer so the marks are at right angles to each other. That is, make the form of a " + " on the top of the wire. This will push the metal outward symmetrically and result in a large, even rivet.

5 As the rivet nears completion, use a small, flat, polished hammer to smooth and shape it. Further shaping can be done with a *beading punch*, a *cup bur* or sandpaper.

4 Elevate the piece slightly so the wire projects from both sides; tap lightly.

5 Drill the second hole, taking care that the elements have not pivoted.

6 Rivets can be shaped with a cup bur (right) or beading tool (here, made from a nail).

FINISHING RIVET HEADS

Because rivets are formed with a hammer, it stands to reason they will show hammer marks. In some cases, these random marks contribute to a design, and may even be exaggerated with stamping tools. Another alternative is to shape the rivet heads into delicate symmetrical domes. This can be done with careful use of files and sandpaper, but when more than a couple of rivets need finishing, use a cup bur or beading punch, or both.

Beading punches are short steel rods, usually only a couple of inches long, with a polished hemispherical depression in one end. They are used primarily to harden and shape the tips of prongs in stone setting and are, unfortunately, too small for some rivets. To make a larger beading tool, saw the point off a steel carpenter's nail and use a drill bit or a *ball bur* to create a depression in the sawn end.

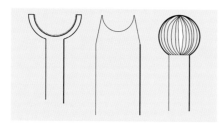

Left to right: cup bur, beading punch, ball bur.

Beading tools can be used manually or with a drill press or electric drill. Either way, rotate the tool aggressively while rocking it back and forth. Use a tool that is slightly smaller than the rivet head: in this way it will not scratch the jewelry even when it is rocked side to side. Many people recommend lubricating the action with a tiny bit of wax or oil.

A cup bur is a steel tool with teeth that remove metal. Unlike beading tools, these are almost impossible to make yourself. They

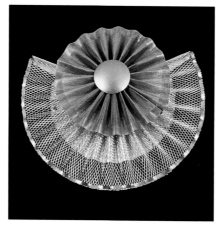

Arline Fisch, *Pleated Mesh*. Sterling, 18K, stainless mesh. 4½ x 4".

work by cutting away excess metal to leave a uniform dome, which can then be polished with a beading punch, sandpaper or buff.

Specialty Rivets

Disappearing (Invisible) Rivets

This variation is made just like a standard rivet, but the material being joined is prepared differently. Holes are drilled in the usual way, but before riveting, the edge of the hole is beveled with a file or bur to create a funnel-shaped opening. Riveting proceeds as usual, but in this case the lump of metal that is upset fills the opening, so that the rivet head is formed flush with the surface. Any excess material can be filed away without danger of weakening the rivet. If the rivet wire is of a contrasting color, say, a copper rivet in a sterling sheet, the result is a dot of inlaid color. If the rivet is made of the same material as the

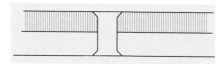

Invisible rivet.

top piece, the rivet will blend into the sheet with the usual finishing steps. Hence the name: disappearing. Amaze your friends!

Tube Rivets

This variation is recommended when joining a fragile material such as enamel, shell or ceramic, because it involves less tapping than a conventional rivet. It also has the advantage of leaving an opening in a piece that can be used for either ornamentation or for a functional requirement like hanging a pendant.

The idea is simple: Instead of a solid wire, a section of tubing is used to make the rivet. Copper and brass tubes can be purchased at a hobby shop, and most suppliers of sterling and gold sheet also sell a few sizes of tubing. If you have a drawplate, it's not difficult to make your own tubing, as explained in Chapter 7.

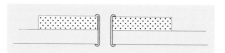

Tube rivet.

As before, holes are drilled carefully and must be a snug fit. The tube is annealed and slipped into position, then trimmed at the same length as a standard rivet. Here's where the similarity ends. With the rivet in position, insert a scribe or similar pointed steel object into the neck of the tube and twirl it around to curl the lip of the tube outward. Flip the work over and repeat the process on the reverse side, continuing until the tube starts to flare out like the bell of a trumpet.

Grasp a dapping punch vertically in the jaws of a vise. Sandwich the rivet between this and another, similar, punch on top. This process is easiest if someone holds the work for you as you manipulate the tools and a hammer. Tap lightly to curl the rivet outward and cinch it tight. If you don't have the correct size dapping punch, it's easy enough to file a chamfer or bevel on a steel rod (e.g., a nail), which will do the same thing. Tap on the rivet just until it seats against the workpiece, to avoid stressing the pieces being joined.

Nailhead Rivets

This variation calls for an extra step as the rivet is prepared, and results in a rivet head that is either larger than usual, or requires no hammering, or both. Start by selecting a wire as before, and drill a hole that makes a snug fit. Draw a bead on the wire by holding it vertically into a flame, taking care to withdraw the flame slowly so as to ensure a smooth surface. Quench the wire in water and dry it off.

David and Roberta Williamson, *Fitz* pin. Sterling, found objects. 3 x 2½".

TUBE RIVET

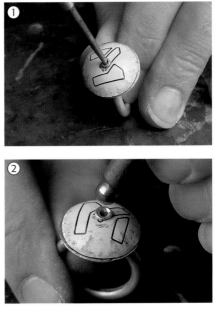

1 Rotate a scribe in the mouth of the tube to bend it outward.

2 Gentle tapping with a rounded punch will curl the lip out and down.

The next step typically uses a drawplate, but you can also make the tool you need by drilling a hole the same diameter as the wire in an eighth-inch or thicker piece of steel. Rest this jig, or a drawplate facing right side up, on the slightly opened jaws of a vise, and slide the wire into the hole until the balled-up end sits against the plate. Use a light hammer to flatten the bead, and you'll have what looks like a nail. This rivet is finished in the conventional way, but has the advantage of having one end preformed. This makes it useful for situations when access to one end of a rivet is difficult. Because the head is larger than usual, a nailhead rivet lends itself to being textured, shaped or ornamented.

Square Rivets

A single rivet allows elements to pivot, which is, of course, sometimes desirable. In those cases where the pieces must remain stable, the usual solution is to use at least two rivets. An alternate method is to make the rivet from square or rectangular wire. Everything proceeds as described above, except that the hole is pierced with a saw and refined with a file to make a snug fit on the rivet.

Washers

When joining two rigid materials—say metal and shell—a couple of rivets are enough to make a solid connection. But when attaching a soft material such as leather, use washers to increase holding power.

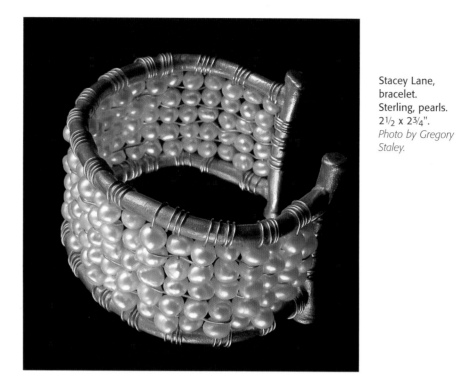

Stacey Lane, bracelet. Sterling, pearls. 2½ x 2¾". *Photo by Gregory Staley.*

individually or in sets. Hardware stores carry sizes down to ¹/₁₆" (1.5 mm); jewelry suppliers can provide much smaller sizes. Taps and dies are sold with special handles that are worth buying if you plan to use them often.

The first step in using a tap is to drill exactly the correct size hole. Charts provided with the tap will tell you which drill bit to use. Once the hole is drilled, grip the metal firmly (e.g., in a vise) and screw the tap into the hole, using a forward-and-reverse motion; this will clear the tiny chips being cut as you go. Turn clockwise a half turn, then counter clockwise a quarter turn, always keeping the tap perpendicular to the sheet. Don't rush it, and don't use much force. Just guide the tool along until it spins easily in your hand.

When threading a rod, it's again important to start with raw material of a correct size. Dies are brittle and will break if you try to thread an oversized rod. Use a file if nec-

We all know what washers look like: disks of steel with a round hole in the center. Well, when it comes to jewelry, forget that. They can be steel, but they can also be gold. They can be smooth, round and symmetrical, or they can be highly integrated ornamental elements. Once the washer is in place, the process is exactly the same as above, and the decorative potential is enormous.

Threaded Connections

The easiest kinds of threaded connections to buy and use are small nuts and bolts from your local hardware store. You'll find them in brass, steel and stainless steel, all of which can be used for jewelry. Smaller bolts are often available through hobby shops, especially those that supply model train enthusiasts. Any of these metals can be soldered using the same flux

and solders mentioned in the last chapter, but if you use steel, do not put the piece in pickle. It can be rinsed in very hot water to dissolve the flux, then cleaned with Scotch-Brite.

The advantage of using bolts to hold pieces together is that the elements can be removed—handy if repairs or cleaning are necessary. The disadvantage is the possibility that the nut might wiggle loose as a piece is worn. One way to guard against this is to put a tiny drop of glue into the nut after assembly. The bond can be broken with a sharp twist if the nut needs to be unscrewed. Alternately, strike the nut with a steel hammer while it sits on an anvil or similar support—this will crimp it slightly, making it more difficult to turn, both going on and coming off.

To cut your own threads you'll need a *tap* and *die*. These tools cut internal and external threads respectively, and can be purchased

j.e. Paterak, pendant. Sterling, 14K engagement ring, mica, moonstone, printed paper. 1¼ x 1¼".

Robert Ebendorf, pin. Tin, tintype, tap, coin. 2 x 3".

essary to make the diameter equal to the largest diameter of the screw, which you can determine by measuring the tap. Grip the rod either vertically or horizontally and use the same screw-unscrew motion to guide the die down the rod. Again, make an effort to keep the die perpendicular to the axis of the rod.

Adhesives

It's traditionally considered a sign of poor craftsmanship to use glue—and sometimes it is. If solder or a mechanical connection can be used, that's probably the route to go. But there are cases where adhesives are acceptable, and many instances when adhesives can be used to supplement mechanical joints. Perhaps the best rule of thumb is this: Whatever technique you use, the same high standards of craftsmanship should apply.

Glues are only as strong as the bond they make on the materials you're joining. Clean metal surfaces, with either sandpaper or a solvent like nail polish remover, to ensure an oxide-free surface. Follow manufacturers' directions carefully to guarantee good results. In the case of epoxies, this includes thorough mixing of the two components. Use a tool you can actually grip (not a broken toothpick) and massage the epoxy from several directions for a couple of minutes.

With the cyanoacrylates (Super Glue), bonding is achieved not by drying, but when air is excluded. That's why this glue is not recommended for porous materials, but works so quickly when you pinch your fingers together. Here again the rules of cleanliness apply.

Finishing & Patinas

5

Finishing is not just a matter of creating a bright shine; it involves sensitive decisions about which color, finish and degree of resolution is appropriate for each piece. Sometimes the traditional high polish of silver or gold is desired, sometimes not, but bear in mind that each case deserves individual consideration. The following pages describe a process that systematically flattens a surface to create a mirror-bright shine, but remember that you can stop at any step along the way. Finishing is more than a process: It is an attitude.

Proper finishing begins with the first mark made on a piece of metal, or more correctly, from the first mark *not* made. Store metal separately from tools that might damage it, and think twice before making any permanent impressions. Of course, forming processes such as hammering, sawing and stamping inevitably leave marks; when these are not wanted, the process of finishing gets started in earnest.

Finishing involves a progression from coarse to fine media. With experience you'll develop a sense of flow from one step to the next. The absence of this intuitive understanding can make finishing frustrating for a beginner, but stick with your craft and the understanding will develop.

Andrew Cooperman, *Truss Series #1* brooch. Bronze, 22K, 18K, 14K, opal. 3" diameter.

Aaron Macsai, *Panels of Movement* bracelet. 18K golds, 14K golds, sterling, copper. ⁷⁄₈ x 7".

Most finishing operations involve at least one selection from each of the following groups.

Group I
Medium or coarse files
100-series grit abrasive paper,
    e.g., 100, 120, 140, etc.
    (or 80 μ [microns])
Brightboy or a similar wheel
Planishing hammer

Group II
Fine files
200-series grit abrasive paper,
    e.g., 220, 240, 260, etc. (or 60 μ)
Pumice (cuts faster dampened
    with water)
Bobbing or Lea compound
Scraper

Group III
Fine abrasive paper, e.g., 300, 320,
    360 (or 40 μ)
Dry pumice
Pumice/rubber wheel

White diamond or tripoli
Scotch-Brite or similar nylon pad
Leather stick with compound

Group IV
Brass scratchbrush lubricated with
    soapy water
Rouge
Polishing papers: 600 grit, 15 μ,
    or 0000 crocus
Fine steel wool (0000)
Hand cloth

Abrasive Media

From earliest times, metalworkers have used rocks and sands of different size and hardness to polish metal. That hasn't changed much, though nowadays we do our mining at the local hardware store. One ancient abrasive that is still widely used is *pumice*, a rough, gray rock formed by volcanoes. It is pulverized and sold as a coarse powder at hardware and paint stores, where you'll find it with the furniture refinishing supplies.

Pour some pumice sand into a shallow dish. Hold a completed object over the dish and rub with a handful of pumice, allowing the extra to fall back into the dish. Repeat as necessary to achieve the intended look. Pumice leaves a soft matte finish on sterling and gold, and is coarse enough to soften edges and remove fine scratches. It can be reused indefinitely, and can be mixed with water to make a paste if desired; damp pumice cuts a little faster than dry. Pumice can be used as a preliminary step to other polishing or as a final step by itself.

Another popular natural abrasive is *garnet*, sometimes known as *crocus*. It can be bought on both cloth and paper, the former being useful when finishing a rounded surface like a spoon bowl.

ABRASIVE PAPERS

Naturally occurring grits used in finishing have been supplemented by synthetic materials—most importantly a very tough grit called *silicon carbide*, available on sandpaper through jewelry supply companies and hardware stores. The grit is sized by a system of numbers corresponding to the mesh used to sort the particles. A high number like 400 identifies a very small particle size, while a number like 120 identifies a coarse grit. As a general rule of thumb, you'll want papers in the 100s, 200s and 300s, as well as number 400.

The latest thing in abrasive papers is a high-tech product that

Micki Lippe, *Jungle* earrings. Sterling, 22K. 1½ x 1½".

PREPARING SANDING STICKS

1 Lay masking tape along the edges of a sheet of sandpaper.

2 Score a line with a blunt point to create a crisp bend.

3 Various molding strips provide a range of shapes. Remember to mark the grit.

4 Use plexiglass or masonite to make wide sanding boards. Rub polishing compounds on cotton string to reach into tight corners.

uses particles of a precise grit size. This, along with a plastic backing and improved adhesives to bond the particles, yields a coated stock (the term "sandpaper" no longer applies) that is significantly more aggressive and durable, and yields a finer finish, all the way up to a high shine. Particles in these products are described by micron size (abbreviated as "μ"); the larger the number, the coarser the abrasive. These products cost several times more than conventional abrasive papers, but since they last so long, they work out to be a good value.

For improved control, greater efficiency, and longer wear, abrasive papers should be attached to a stiff backing. Note that while almost any abrasive will accomplish something on metal, sandpapers made for wood or plastic break apart quickly and are therefore not recommended for jewelry making. By contrast, papers made for metal, when used in proper sequence, will last a long time. Many are waterproof and can be rinsed under running water to flush away clogging debris.

ABRASIVE COMPOUNDS

When particles are extremely fine and can no longer be attached to paper, they are mixed with a greasy binder and formed into bricks that are used to coat (or *charge*) felt or fabric buffs. The range of abrasive compounds is large and confusing, but here are a couple of favorites to get you started.

Bobbing
This popular tan-colored compound contains naturally occurring sandstone and is an aggressive abrasive. It will remove scratches and leave a semi-polished surface.

White Diamond
This commercial product contains

David and Roberta Williamson, *Welcome* pin. Sterling, copper, found object. 3 x 1¼".

no diamond, but is nevertheless a very fast cutting agent. It leaves a brighter shine than bobbing.

Rouge

This also contains a naturally occurring compound—iron oxide, better known as rust. Rouge does not remove material, but burnishes a surface to create a warm shine.

Burnishing Media

Burnishing is distinguished from abrading in that no material is removed. Instead, the surface is rubbed with a hard tool that pushes the raised areas down, flattening the "peaks" into the "valleys" to create a smooth, reflective surface. This ancient technique uses polished tools of brass, bronze, steel and stone. A modern process called tumbling uses steel shot (which looks like BBs) in a rotating or vibrating drum to achieve a similar effect.

HAND BURNISHING

A burnishing tool is nothing more than a comfortable handle fitted with a short, tapered steel rod about the size of your little finger. To work properly it must remain highly polished; wrap it in an oiled cloth when not in use to protect against rust. A burnisher can be made from any piece of steel; a satisfactory tool can be made by cutting the tip from a screwdriver and rounding the end.

To use a burnisher, rub the tool over a surface, pressing down firmly and moving the tool in several directions. A light lubricant such as saliva or a fine oil is typically used. Most important, don't rely on burnishing to alter surface contour.

For instance, if you want a surface flat and shiny, make it flat with files and sandpaper, then turn to the burnisher to make it shiny. Burnishing an uneven surface will create a shiny uneven surface.

A *polishing stick* uses leather imbedded with rouge. While slower than machine buffing, this method is nevertheless very effective and provides great control.

To make a polishing stick, glue a piece of leather firmly onto a straight flat stick about a foot long and an inch wide. Use epoxy or hide glue and weight the assembly to be certain the leather is attached all the way to its edges. The leather can be either smooth or suede and doesn't need to be anything fancy; I usually use belts or purse straps from used-clothing stores. Once the glue has set, rub rouge or any other compound into the leather. Use a different stick for each abra-

Dawn Eileen Nakanishi, *Flotation* brooch. Sterling, 14K. 4 x 5". *Photo by Helen Shirk.*

sive, recharging as necessary. Polishing sticks are usually used like sanding sticks—rubbed against the work as it is supported by the bench pin. For small objects, it's also possible to set the stick down on the bench top and rub the piece against it.

Scratch Brushing

This popular tool has bristles of thin brass or stainless steel wire, and is used to develop a soft glowing shine. Use a brass brush on gold, silver, copper or brass, reserving the less versatile steel brush for nickel silver and steel. In all cases, use soapy water to lubricate the burnishing action. Rub the brush on a cake of soap, dip it into a pan of suds, or dribble a line of dishwashing detergent on the bristles, and work at the sink in a trickle of water. Scrub the work in all directions, continuing until the desired shine is achieved.

Scratch brushes are also made for use with both flexible shaft and bench-mounted polishing motors. In both cases, care should be taken to run at slower speeds than with other kinds of polishing. With the flex shaft this can be done by careful control of the foot pedal that controls speed, but a fixed rpm motor will need to be outfitted with a pair of V-wheels and a belt to reduce the speed to around 800 rpm. This is not as difficult as it might sound—seek help from a local industrial supplier.

Machine Finishing

It is entirely possible to get excellent results through hand finishing, but many jewelers use machines, especially when the goal is a high polish. For most polishing, you can use either a bench-mounted motor, usually 1725 rpm or faster, or the smaller bench-side machine called a flexible shaft. But before describing specifics, it's worthwhile to discuss safety.

Given the chance, a buffing machine will snag long hair or loose clothing, with disastrous consequences. If the machine grabs something, you simply do not have time to respond. It is therefore critical to always keep hair tied back and remove jewelry, scarves, etc. Follow this rule without exception!

Buffing machines throw up a lot of grit and dust. Wear goggles and protect your lungs and nasal passages with a respirator. The best device is one fitted with appropriate, disposable cartridges, but at the very least, wear a disposable paper mask. Replace the paper mask or cartridge as soon as it becomes saturated with dust.

Always grip work in such a way that it can be pulled from your hands with little resistance. The opposite of this would be to put a ring on your finger, or to grasp a bracelet by sliding your fingers through the piece. If the spinning buff snags on the piece in these situations, your hand is at risk of serious injury.

If you do not intend to follow these important guidelines, do not use a buffing machine.

Flexible Shaft Machine

This popular and versatile tool is used for polishing. It also comes in handy for drilling holes, setting stones, grinding off rough edges, and carving soft materials. The complete machine includes a precision motor, a flexible shaft with handpiece, and a foot rheostat to provide variable speed. Tools for the flex shaft, called *mandrels*, are made in a dizzying collection of styles. Consult a jewelry supply catalog for details and plan on experimenting to find the ones that work best for you. In some cases the working part of the tool, such as a grinding wheel or brass brush, might be permanently bonded to the shaft of the mandrel. Other tools, like muslin buffs or sanding disks, are sold separately and can be replaced as they wear out.

Buffing Machines

The ideal machine for buffing is sealed to protect it from dust and grit, but unsealed motors are commonly used too, especially since they are a lot cheaper and easier to acquire. The best motor for polishing runs at 1725 revolutions per minute (rpm) and is 1/4 horsepower in strength. Conveniently for us, that's the motor used in washing machines, refrigerators, furnaces, and clothes dryers—which is to say, there are a lot of them out there. Used motors are available from appliance repair companies, and new motors are sold through jewelry suppliers.

Either a single or double spindle motor can be used, and should be mounted at a comfortable height on a sturdy table or counter. Buffs are available in many sizes, with 6" diameter being the most popular. To provide clearance between the edge of the buff and the tabletop, mount the motor so the spindle is at least 5" above the surface.

The motor must be situated so the direction of rotation is down and away from the worker. Measure the spindle diameter and order an attachment called a *threaded tapered spindle*, being careful to specify spindle diameter (usually $1/2$" or $5/8$"), as well as the side of the motor—left or right. This adapter allows various buffs to be quickly fitted onto the machine. It is designed to tighten the hold of the buff as it is used, which is why it is side-specific. If a right-hand tapered spindle is used on a left-hand machine, buffs will loosen and fly off as soon as a piece is brought into contact.

To catch the dust of machine buffing, make or buy a polishing hood to set behind the wheel. In a light-use situation, this can be as simple as a box to catch flying lint and particles, but a much better solution is to attach a vacuum cleaner to the outlet of this hood. This will not only prevent dust from filling the air, but will collect the dust for reclamation. In the case of gold, even an expensive system will pay for itself quickly as scrap is refined.

A bead held against a muslin buffing wheel.

USES OF THE FLEXIBLE SHAFT

1 Drilling.
2 Sanding.

3 Carving.
4 Grinding.

5 Stone setting.
6 Buffing.

Deborah Krupenia,
E III Brooch.
Colored golds, fine silver,
Japanese copper alloys,
sterling. 3³⁄₈ x 2³⁄₄".
Photo by Dean Powell.

Buffs and Attachments

In the case of sandpaper, we can easily visualize the two elements involved: sand and paper, one doing the cutting and the other carrying the grit to the piece. The same concept is at work in machine buffing, but the carrier is usually made of fabric and shaped like an oversized hockey puck. Here again, a glance at a catalog might confound you with the range of buffs available. Take heart. For most studios and situations, a couple of basic buffs will suffice.

You will need at least two separate buffs for each compound, usually one made of felt and one of muslin. A muslin buff is made of disks of coarse fabric stacked up and stitched together. Buffs are typically described by diameter (in inches) and the number of layers, with 50 or 60 layers of fabric being most popular. A 6" wheel is a good all purpose starter, and will soon wear down to become smaller and therefore useful for reaching into tight areas. Even with the speed of the motor constant, the size of the wheel determines the surface feet per minute (sfm), which, in turn, determines how fast a wheel cuts. The larger the wheel, the faster it will cut.

Muslin wheels are used to remove scratches, round off edges, and increase shine. They have the ability to blend elements together and, used sparingly, tend to homogenize a piece. That's good. When overused, however, muslin buffs wear down detail, erode textures and generally take the life out of a piece. That's bad. Only experience will clarify the uses of each buff and compound, but you can accelerate your learning by paying close attention to the results you get in every instance.

Before its first use, a muslin buff should be raked to remove some of its lint. This will come off in the first 10 minutes of use anyway, so you might as well get the shedding done before starting to work. Use an old kitchen fork, or make a rake by driving a dozen nails through the last 2 inches of a 10-inch strip of wood. Put on goggles and a respirator, and with the buff mounted and spinning on the machine, hold the rake against the wheel for a

Thomas Mann,
*Rusted Wire Frame
Wheel with Stone.*
Steel, stone.
3³⁄₄" diameter.
*Photo by Gerard
Perrone.*

couple of minutes. Both lint and loose threads will be pulled from the buff. Stop the wheel and use scissors to trim the threads. Now you can charge the buff with compound and put it into use. Remember to mark each buff clearly so you won't contaminate it with the wrong compound.

Felt buffs are similar to muslin in size and shape, but are much more dense, and less likely to drape themselves over a surface. For this reason they are preferred for angular pieces, and when the polishing action needs to be confined to an isolated area. Felt buffs do not need to be raked like their muslin cousins, but they sometimes cake solid on their outer circumference and need to be scraped clean. To achieve this, have the buff running on the motor and hold a flat piece of scrap steel perpendicular to the wheel. Of course, goggles and a respirator should be worn for this.

Robert Ebendorf, ring. 18K, iron wire, diamond.

To Glove or Not to Glove

Buffing is a hot, dirty business—no way around it. To protect against the heat of friction, and to minimize the tenacious smudge that will penetrate skin, some people like to wear cloth gardening gloves when buffing. These accomplish the protection they promise, but make the wearer's grip clumsy and insensitive. It's a matter of taste and experience. I don't wear gloves because I want to know how hot the metal is getting, and I like to "steer" the work against the wheel with subtle movements that gloves make difficult. A useful middle course is to use medical-style rubber gloves. These don't protect against heat, but they will keep your hands clean.

Applying Compound

Think of a buffing wheel as sandpaper that you keep renewing. The compound is scraped off the wheel as it rubs against metal, but you have the opportunity to renew it as needed. With the motor running, hold the bar of compound firmly against the wheel for a second to load it. At 1725 rpm, a buff rotates almost 30 times in that second, so it doesn't take long to expose the circumference of the wheel to all the compound it can hold. Applying more is simply going to make a mess as the excess compound falls off. Better to reapply every couple of minutes than overdo it at a single charging.

Clean Up

Because the binder in compounds is a mixture of grease and wax, it takes more than just a light pass through the sink to clean your hands after polishing. Combine a small amount of ammonia with liquid soap, like dishwashing detergent, and thin this with water. The proportions are not important, but this is the mix that will cut the compounds. Drop the piece in a dish of this mixture to soak for a few minutes while you use some more to clean your hands. Then use a toothbrush and the soapy mix to scrub the work, continuing until the soap foam is no longer colored by the compound. Rinse and dry the work. It's important to clean a piece after each stage of polishing to prevent contamination of the wheels.

Now that you've got that piece sparkling bright and free of all the compounds it picked up during polishing, you dry it on a fuzzy towel, right? Not right—unless you want your work to turn into Chia Jewelry. Lint from a cloth will grab onto textures you didn't even know you had, so find another solution!

Air drying is not ideal, since it can leave water spots. A time-honored method of drying jewelry is to toss it into a box of fine sawdust (available from any woodshop). After a few minutes, you can pull it out and blow to remove any clinging sawdust. Another method is to set the work on a cloth and dry it with a hair dryer; turn the work as needed to expose each surface. This method doesn't have the medieval charm of sawdust drying, but it's faster!

Patinas

It's hard to beat the warm, lustrous beauty of polished metal—hard, but not impossible. In addition to its ability to achieve a highly reflective shine, metal offers a wealth of color options through the formation of colored layers we call patinas. In reality, patinas are usually corrosion products (not nearly as pleasant-sounding) and are the result of chemical activity on the metal surface. We see patinas all around us, from rusty machinery to crusty green statues on the town square. These are typically caused by a slow, natural process. In the studio, the chemical reaction is usually the same. We just take the place of weather and pollution to create more or less predictable—and accelerated—results.

The color achieved by a specific patina solution will depend on the alloy to which it's applied, the age and strength of the mixture, the time and temperature of the exposure, and the process used to apply the solution.

Depending upon your frame of mind, the interaction of these factors can add up to an exciting discovery or a huge frustration. If you approach patinas in the spirit of selecting paint swatches—anticipating uniform colors and consistent results—you are bound to be disappointed. But when you realize that patinas are the result of a progressive chemical action, a sort of "living thing," you open yourself to exciting possibilities.

Let's focus on the three fundamental elements of patinas: application methods, recipes, and variables. In the end your results will depend on the interaction of these ingredients.

APPLICATION METHODS

Probably the most common application method, at least for jewelry-sized work, is to simply drop the piece into a container of the appropriate solution. Sounds easy, right? Well, it is, but there are a few important tips to bear in mind.

With all patina applications, clean metal is very important. Once the work is free of grease and oxides, avoid touching it with your fingers. Secure each piece with a wire handle so you can lower it into the bath efficiently.

In many cases, it's helpful to have the work slightly warm. I accomplish this by holding the piece (in its wire handle) under hot running tap water before plunging it into the patina solution. It is usually wise to develop a patina slowly—with several immersions of just a few seconds each—partly because

PATINA APPLICATION METHODS

To contain a piece in a fuming environment, either set it above a pool of solution or hang it from a lid with string and tape. To create a random speckled pattern, bury pieces in sawdust that has been saturated with patina solution.

Patricia Telesco,
Series XXVI, #1
brooch. Bronze,
nickel, 18K, 14K.
2 x 2".
*Photo by Charlie
Seifried.*

you can see the various stages of color transition, and partly because a color developed slowly is usually more permanent. The sequence should be: warm, dip, rinse. Repeat this as many as a dozen times to achieve the color you want.

Spray

Use a spray bottle from the drugstore to lightly spritz patina chemicals onto a clean surface. Gravity being what it is, this method can also be used with some solutions to develop drip patterns. To contain the overspray, set the work in a disposable cardboard box.

Heat

Heating metal with a torch will create patina, but the process is usually difficult to control. One specific heat patina—copper in an oven—is an exception and worth describing. After all soldering, texturing and filing have been completed, clean the piece thoroughly in soapy water, rinse it, dry it, and set it in a standard kitchen oven set at 350°F. Check it every 10 minutes, and you'll see the surface go from a lustrous nutty brown to a brilliant crimson, and eventually to bright blue. The patina usually takes about 20-30 minutes, though both the time and temperature vary depending on the kind of oven and the size of the piece. When the correct patina has been achieved, remove the piece and allow it to air cool. This finish is fragile and not recommended for bracelets or oth-

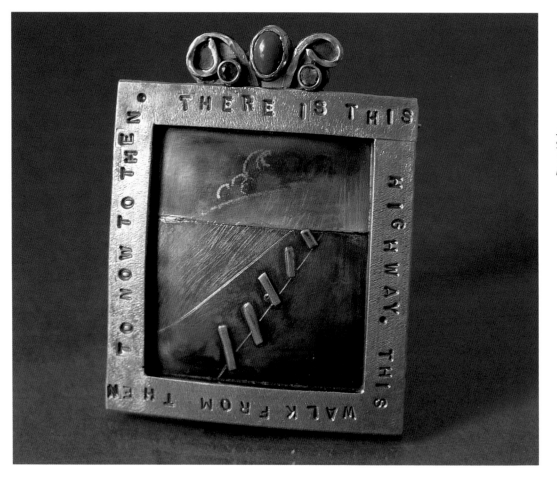

Jenepher Burton, brooch.
Sterling, copper, brass,
18K, turquoise. 2 x 2½".
Photo by Robert Diamante.

er jewelry that will get a lot of wear, but I've had good luck with earrings and brooches, especially if they've been stored in plastic bags when not being worn.

Atmosphere

The wonderful patinas we see on copper drain spouts and outdoor statuary are the result of a delicate attack by airborne vapors. It's a situation we can recreate in the studio with a container or a plastic bag. Begin by setting a small dish of the patina chemical (e.g., ammonia) in an out-of-the-way place, preferably in a warm spot since heat accelerates most corrosive reactions. Have your clean metal piece nearby, ideally suspended above the dish of solution, then cover the arrangement with a bucket or a draped plastic sheet. A transparent material has the advantage of allowing you to assess progress of the patina without disturbing the environment.

Within this environment, the atmosphere will thicken with fumes from the dish of solution, and the fumes will condense on the metal object and work their magic. Space, materials, and the shape of your piece all influence the result. Depending on the alloy, the solution and the weather, you may wait as long as several days for the patina to develop.

Burying

In this case an absorbent granular material is saturated with a patina solution and used to completely surround a metal object. A typical situation is a plastic bag of sawdust, stirred until evenly moist with a solution like the one for Green Patina (see the recipe on page 66).

When the sawdust is uniformly dampened, push a piece into the center of the mass and tightly seal up the bag. Now comes the hard part: don't disturb it for several days. When you can't take the suspense any longer, open the bag to check the progress. You will probably see a speckled pattern, the result of separate bits of sawdust coming into direct contact with the metal and holding the patina solution against the surface. For this reason, different size chips or particles will have dramatically different results. Other surrounding materials include dried leaves, cat litter, and shredded paper.

PATINA SOLUTIONS

Over the centuries, metalsmiths have developed hundreds, maybe thousands, of recipes for patina solutions. To do these recipes justice would take several volumes—each larger than this one—and more knowledge of chemistry than I have. But with the understanding that even a few formulas will provide a wide range of options, let's proceed. I've ruled out solutions that involve dangerous, expensive or rare chemicals, and present only those with the highest rate of success, the sure-fire winners.

Patina Safety

- Mark patina containers clearly.
- Keep solutions safely stored away from children and pets.
- Wear rubber gloves and goggles when using strong chemicals.
- Use ventilation when applying patinas.

Liver of Sulfur on Sterling

This is perhaps the most widely used patina chemical among jewelers who work in sterling silver. For the best results, mix a fresh solution of liver of sulfur for every use. It's usually sold in the form of gravel, but sometimes comes ready-to-use as an amber-colored liquid.

Liver of sulfur (potassium sulfide) breaks down when exposed to air or light, so keep it tightly sealed in an opaque container. If purchased dry, be careful that no moisture or air enters the jar. If you spill a drop of water or leave the top off overnight, the batch will soon be useless.

Liver of sulfur is used through immersion. Clean your finished piece and hold it under hot running tap water, then drop it into a container of liver of sulfur solution. Though the mixture smells foul, it is not toxic at room temper-

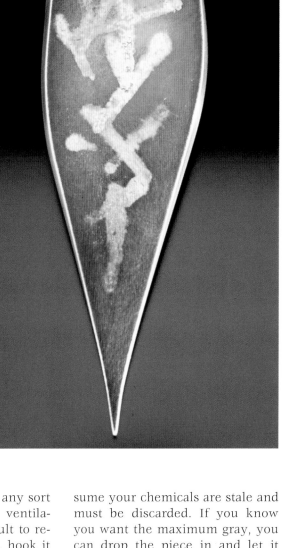

John Cogswell, *Shield Brooch*. Sterling, 14K. 4 x 1½".

ature, and can be used in any sort of container and without ventilation. If the piece is difficult to retrieve from the container, hook it onto a scrap of wire so you can suspend it in the bath and remove it promptly.

If the mix is fresh, sterling will turn dark gray in about a minute. A weak or over-strong solution will take perhaps twice that long. If nothing is happening by then, as-

sume your chemicals are stale and must be discarded. If you know you want the maximum gray, you can drop the piece in and let it soak. However, a better approach, is to dip the piece quickly, then rinse it in running water to check the effect. Before turning gray, sterling progresses through these colors: yellow, brown, crimson, and electric blue. Though none are as durable as the gray, these colors can last quite a while on pins and earrings, and are worth considering. Dip and rinse repeatedly, until the work achieves the desired color, then give a thorough rinse in running water to remove every trace of liver of sulfur.

To darken selected areas, first make the entire piece gray, then use pumice or a polishing compound to remove the patina from raised areas. If you darken a piece and don't like the result, heat the piece slightly with a torch, then drop it in warm pickle.

Green Patina on Copper

1 tablespoon ammonium chloride (sal ammoniac)
1 tablespoon salt
1 ounce plain ammonia
1 quart water

Mix these chemicals in a plastic container and mark it clearly so it will never be confused with food. Warm water speeds the dissolving, but cool water can be used. If local tap water is laced with minerals, use bottled water. The mixture is colorless, but you might want to add a couple of drops of green food color to make the chemical easily recognizable.

This compound, unlike liver of sulfur, takes a while to show its effects. Clean the item and set it in an isolated area, preferably one with some light ventilation and warm air. Brush or spray the solution on to achieve a thin coating. The piece will look wet, but nothing more dramatic will occur. Allow the piece to dry naturally, after which you might see a pale gray film starting to form. Brush or spray the piece again (which will "erase" what little patina you had), and again allow the piece to air dry. Repeat this process for at least five cycles to create a lichen-colored green crust.

It's tempting to accelerate the process by drying the piece with a

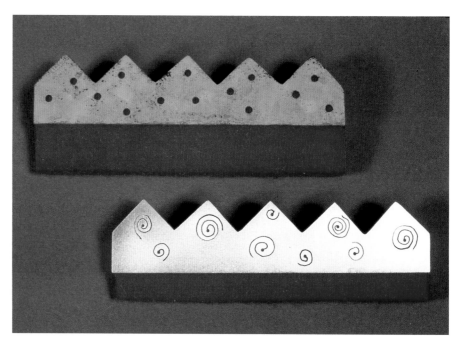

Cynthia Cetlin, *Architectural Brooch Series*. Red felt, patinated copper. 1½ x 3¼".
Photo by Jonathan Quick.

torch or a hair dryer. Don't. The green crust that forms in this way will not be bonded to the copper beneath it and will wipe off at the lightest touch. Be patient and do it right, which means 24 to 48 hours, depending on weather conditions. To increase the blue tones, increase the amount of salt in the solution, or sprinkle salt directly onto the wet surface.

Gun Bluing on Steel, Brass or Bronze

This commercial product is used to create a patina on firearms, which are, of course, made of steel. It can be purchased in sporting goods stores, and, like liver of sulfur, gives immediate results. To achieve a deep blue-black on steel, simply follow the directions. To create a purple-gray on brass or bronze, use the solution straight from the bottle. Apply with a bit of steel wool, either held in the hands or as a small pad gripped with tweezers. To color a delicate object like a

chain, pour some gun bluing into a small dish and toss in some bits of steel—nails, staples or paper clips will work. Immerse the piece for a few minutes, then flush it well in running water.

SEALING PATINAS

As mentioned, patinas are the result of air, air-borne chemicals, and moisture, all interacting chemically with metals. As long as the piece is exposed to air, the action is likely to continue. Again, this can be an exciting part of the process or a frustration, depending on your attitude. Steps can be taken to protect a patina, but they are best viewed as retarding—rather than halting—a natural process of corrosion.

Sealing a patina from the atmosphere has an inherent problem in that you must inevitably add a layer of something to the patina. Even if what you add is perfectly clear, it will alter the way light is reflected,

Deborah Krupenia,
*Mismatched Fazzoletti II
Earrings.*
Colored golds, Japanese
copper alloys, sterling.
Photo by Dean Powell.

which is the essence of color perception. As a result, a piece that was a bright blue might appear as a dull purple.

Patina coatings fall into two categories—hard and soft. Hard coatings, like lacquer, are strong and effective, but can chip if the metal is flexed or bumped. Soft coatings, like wax, move with the metal, but eventually rub off, not only leaving the patina exposed, but possibly staining a garment in the process.

Spray lacquer is available from art supply companies; look for the light-duty variety used to protect charcoal and pastel drawings. Set or suspend the work in a well-ventilated area and spray a thin coating following the directions on the can. Resist the urge to spray too much, because the excess will drip. Allow the work to dry, which might take only a few minutes, and repeat the process. At least five layers will be needed to protect a patina.

Car wax can be used to protect a patina, but a gentler wax used for furniture protection offers a better solution. This can be found at hardware stores (one brand is called Butchers Wax). Apply the wax with a soft cloth and allow it to dry for a few minutes, then gently wipe it off. This step can be alarming in the case of green patina, which often starts to come off on the cloth. If the patina was properly developed, though, there will be enough remaining to color the piece. To make the wax easier to apply, warm the work slightly with a hair dryer at the start of the process, or work in a sunny spot.

6

Stone Setting

From its earliest origins, jewelry has been linked to the incredible bounty of the earth, especially gemstones, which have long been associated with magical properties, healing power and wealth. Of course, it's possible to make jewelry without gemstones, but who would want to!

Because most gems will not withstand the heat of soldering, the techniques described in this chapter are specific kinds of cold connections. We'll take a look at the categories of gemstones and describe a few of the most popular setting styles, but here again an innovative jeweler will take these standard settings as a starting point for his or her own ideas.

A Word About Gemstones

The art of cutting and polishing gems is called *lapidary*, and is a rich and rewarding field all by itself. Gems are usually mineral materials formed in the earth through the actions of chemicals, water, pressure and heat, and as we know, they present a wealth of color and pattern. Some organic (once-living) materials, such as coral, amber and pearls, are also considered gems.

This natural trove has been augmented by synthetic stones and, not surprisingly, the range of these has only increased with advanced

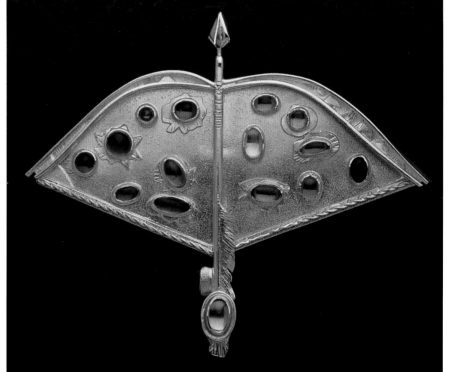

Stephani Briggs, *Pathfinder* pin/pendant. 22K, 18K, Maine tourmalines. 3 x 4".

technology. Synthetic stones are sometimes frowned upon for serious jewelry. This is true, for example, with synthetic garnets and amethysts; the natural stones are both readily available and not significantly more expensive than their synthetic counterparts. In other cases, as with emeralds and diamonds, synthetics are more

generally accepted. Whenever a synthetic is used, any reference to the gem must make its origin clear.

A full description of gemology is outside the scope of this book, but as you pursue jewelry making, you'll want to familiarize yourself with the names and qualities of stones. You'll also learn about color variations, hardness and idiosyncrasies that contribute to the value of a gem. Gradually you'll select some favorites and decide which stones lend themselves to your work. You can start by reading the captions in this book to learn the names of a few stones you might not have seen before.

TYPES OF STONES

Since our earliest ancestors picked up brightly colored rocks along the beach, people have been shaping, polishing and collecting stones. While lapidary is a complex art, for our purposes we can divide the universe of cut stones into three broad categories: *tumbled, cabochon* and *faceted*.

Tumbled

These stones are free-form lumps that are mass-finished by tumbling them in a drum with water and abrasive particles. They can be pretty, but are difficult to set well.

Cabochon

These stones are smooth, convex forms, usually with flat undersides. They may be round, oval, square or any other shape when viewed from the top, but from the side they take the shape of a rounded mound. Some translucent (see-through) stones are cut as cabochons, but most stones cut this way are opaque. This name is typically shortened to *cab*.

Faceted

A facet, or face, is a small flat plane cut on a stone. Facets are arranged geometrically over the entire surface of a transparent or translucent gem to focus light into the stone and reflect it back. All of this enhances the natural sparkle of the stone, which can be round, oval or any of dozens of other shapes. Faceted stones are no more difficult to set than cabs, though they

Tumbled, cabochon and faceted stones.

Tom Herman, earrings. Lapis, pearls, 18K. 2½ x ¾".

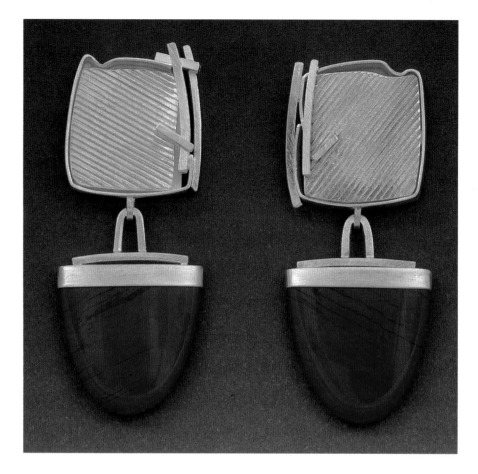

Micki Lippe, earrings.
Sterling, 22K, red jasper. 3 x 3".

usually require precision to properly complement the extreme geometry of the cut.

In order to understand the directions that follow, you'll need to know the parts of a faceted stone, as shown in the diagram here. The widest part is called the *girdle*, the area above the girdle is the *crown*, and the area below is called the *pavilion*. The flat surface on the top is the *table* and the point at the very bottom is the *culet*.

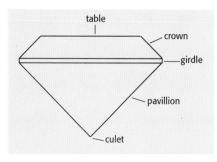

Stone Setting Guidelines

- The stone must be securely held.
- The setting should complement the stone.
- The setting must not snag on clothing or hair.
- The setting should relate to the piece around it.

Basic Bezels

A bezel is a strip of metal that surrounds a stone and is pressed down over its sloping contour to secure it in place. A bezel is constructed as a thin, low wall that stands vertically, and perfectly encases the stone. After all soldering and finishing is complete, the stone is placed into position and the bezel is pressed against it. All suppliers of precious

metals sell strips of fine silver and gold called *bezel wire*. While these are a convenient size and shape for stone setting, don't neglect the opportunities presented by using other stock to make bezels.

Bezels can be made from any of the usual jewelry metals (gold, sterling, silver, copper and brass) and can be thick or thin, plain or decorated. They can be cut from sheet stock, hammered from wire or purchased as ready-made bezel strip. Bezels are almost always used for cabochons, but they work well on faceted stones too. In order to lift the culet, faceted stones usually require a tall bezel with an inner step or ledge.

Bezel wire is shown in the photo sequence starting on page 72, where it is used on a sterling base to make a *box bezel*—a solid-backed container that holds the stone. A variation known as *shelf* or *ledge bezel* is a strip of metal that is thinner at the very top, with an inner ledge where the stone can rest. In this case no sheet is needed below the stone, which means weight and cost of the setting are reduced. Because the ledge is small, this method requires careful fitting, and is not recommended for large stones or for situations—as with a ring—where the setting might take a lot of stress.

Another variation, called *gallery wire*, is bezel wire decorated with an ornamental pattern. Both shelf bezel and gallery wire were originally made by hand for each project and setting, and of course that can still be done. Fancy commercial bezels can be very attractive, although overuse tends to make them less appealing.

Making a Box Bezel

1 Fit the bezel to the stone.
2 Solder on a backing, trim and clean the seam.
3 Adjust the height of the bezel walls.
4 Set the stone.
5 Smooth and shape the bezel.

Fit the bezel to the stone. Examine the stone, noting particularly the angle where the flat bottom meets the curving top. This angle, more than anything else, determines the height of the bezel. If you are unfamiliar with the stone, and if the back will be hidden in a box bezel, scratch the flat surface with the tip of a file to determine its hardness.

In the photo sequence starting on page 72, I used commercially purchased eighth-inch bezel wire made of fine silver. I could have made a similar strip by cutting silver sheet or rolling out a wire. Fine silver is used because it's malleable enough to press safely over the stone. Sterling, gold, copper and brass can also be used.

Bend the wire into a loop that will fit snugly around the stone, avoiding kinks and pliers marks. I usually do this by eye, checking it against the stone periodically. Large or asymmetrical stones can be attached to the table with double-stick tape and worked over directly. Proper fit at this stage is critical, so take your time and make it right. When it is, use scissors or wire cutters to snip the bezel, file the ends so they meet neatly, and solder the bezel closed with a tiny piece of hard solder. Solder is significantly less malleable than most bezel materials, so using too much will make a tough section that resists pressing against the stone.

Test the bezel by pressing it gently over the stone. The fit should be like a hand in a glove: the stone shouldn't be difficult to push into the bezel, but once there it should not rattle around. If the bezel is too large, cut a piece out at the seam and resolder. If it is a little too small, put the bezel on a mandrel and slide it along the taper to stretch it. Test frequently so you don't go too far. If the bezel is significantly too small, start over. Either way, don't proceed until you get it right.

The actual setting process—the last step described below—is very easy when the bezel fits well and quite frustrating when it doesn't. Some people ask which is better, too loose or too tight? The answer is *neither*. Time spent making it right at this stage will save twice the time later on, and yield a better setting, as well.

Solder on a backing. When the fit is right, rub the bezel lightly on sand-

Claire Sanford, three pins. Sterling, 22K, stones. 4 to 7" tall.

paper to make its lower edge flat and clean. Check to be certain it hasn't distorted, and set it on a piece of sheet metal just slightly larger than the stone. The thickness of the sheet will depend on the size of the stone, but it doesn't have to be very thick to do its job. Stones under 5 mm might be set on 24-gauge sheet, with large stones needing something like 20-gauge.

Clean the metal with Scotch-Brite and prop it at a slight angle by setting it on a pumice pebble or extra bit of firebrick. This will allow the heat of the torch to reach beneath the sheet and minimize the heat drawn off by the firebrick. Flux the sheet and set the bezel into place so it has a couple of millimeters clearance on all sides. It's typical for the bezel to slide a little during soldering; this allowance will accommodate that. Set two or three pieces of medium solder so they touch both the bezel and the sheet; they can be on either the inside or the outside of the bezel. Remember, it won't take much.

Patty Bolz, brooch. 22K, boulder opal, tsavorite garnets, grossular garnet. 1 x 3½".
Photo by William Thuss Photography.

Heat the assembly uniformly, so the solder flows all the way around the bezel in a single sweeping motion. Keep the torch moving, focusing the flame on the sheet rather than the bezel. As soon as the solder flows, remove the flame, quench the piece in water and then pickle it to remove oxides and flux residue. Pat yourself on the back, but resist the urge to test the stone in position! It fit a minute ago, so you can be pretty confident that it still fits.

MAKING A BOX BEZEL

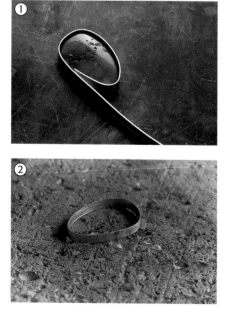

1 Bend a loop of flattened wire around the stone.

2 Solder the bezel closed, using a small piece of hard solder.

3 After testing the fit, solder the bezel to a backing sheet.

4 In this case, wire was added for decoration. Trim away extra sheet.

5 Stamps are used to ornament the wire.

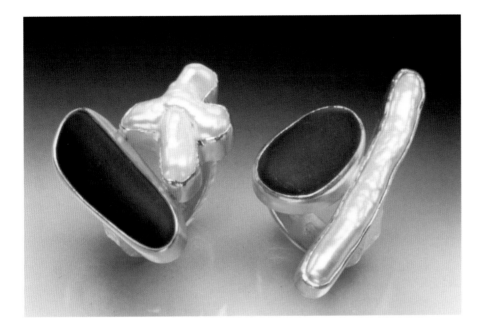

Sam Shaw, two rings. 22K, baroque pearls, beach stones.

Trim the area outside the bezel with a saw or shears. In the example, I left a ledge of metal around the bezel to hold a decorative strip; in most cases the sheet is trimmed flush with the bezel wall. File and sand to make the seam disappear.

At this point, you can attach the bezel to a piece of jewelry, using easy solder. Each situation will dictate its own placement of pieces and solder chips. Throughout these steps, set the gemstone safely out of the way, where it will not get damaged or lost as you complete the assembly.

Adjust the height of the bezel walls. The correct height of a bezel is determined by the height of the stone, the wear the jewelry is likely to take, and the thickness of the bezel. A large, tall stone on a ring, for instance, will need more bezel than a shallow stone on an earring. Shallow stones require less bezel because the metal is pressed over the gem at a sharp angle. Tall stones, on the other hand, have little allowance for the metal to press down on them and, because they are tall, are more likely to be

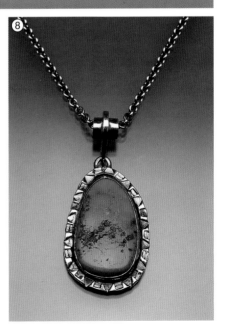

6 Working side-to-side, use a bezel pusher to press the bezel against the stone.

7 The bezel can be smoothed and polished with a pumice wheel, followed by light buffing.

8 The finished piece.

Patty Bolz, earrings. 22K, boulder opals, pink sapphires. *Photo by Robert Diamante.*

bumped. These bezels, therefore, need to be tall and sturdy.

To determine height, lay the stone beside the bezel, remembering to take into account the thickness of the bottom sheet, which will raise the stone slightly. Note the angle of the stone and make a guess about how much bezel will be needed to secure it. Of course, this gets easier with experience. If the bezel is too tall, either trim it down with a file, or raise the stone within the bezel by inserting a loop of wire or a piece of sheet.

After all construction and patination—as well as most polishing—are complete, the stone is pressed into the bezel. Before attempting this, use a blunt tool like the handle of a needle file or a pliers, to roll the bezel wall slightly outward. This simple step might save you a moment of panic. It's common for the bezel to have closed somewhat during the finishing process, and it might at first appear to have shrunk.

Set the stone. Working on a cushioned surface (a folded cloth works well), press the stone into place. Make sure it's seated all the way into the bezel. If it doesn't fit, examine the situation carefully—preferably with magnification—to determine where the trouble lies. Don't do anything until you've identified the problem. Then file, scrape or sand the bezel as necessary to fit the stone.

The tool used to press the bezel onto the stone is called a *bezel pusher*. It is nothing more than a short steel rod set into a comfortable, bulbous handle. Bezel pushers can be purchased or made—a simple version uses a nail pounded into a golf ball and trimmed to a comfortable length. The tip of the bezel pusher should be flat, smooth and slightly textured in order to avoid slipping on the bezel. True it up periodically with medium grit sandpaper.

The trick in setting is to avoid creating a pucker of excess mater-

ial at one spot on the bezel. This will be the result if you move concentrically around the circle, so don't do that. Instead, start by pressing the bezel over the stone at each of the four compass points or, if you imagine the face of a clock, at 3, 6, 9 and 12. It doesn't matter where you start, but use this back and forth method throughout the setting to evenly distribute the compression of the bezel as it leans inward.

After making the first four bends, double check that the stone is level, that the bezel is the right height, and that you have completed all soldering. If you need to remove the stone, use a thin blade to pry the bends back, and pop the stone out by holding the piece in your hand and rapping it with a piece of wood (like a file handle).

If everything is in order, continue the pressing, this time working at spots midway between each of the first four. Continue in this way, always jumping across the stone to address an area opposite the last pressing point. Stick with it until all the bumps have been pressed

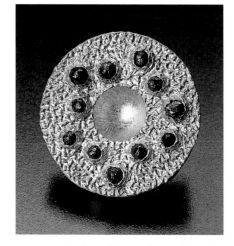

Devta Doolan, brooch. 22K, diamond crystals. 2" diameter.
Photo by Robert Diamante.

Kristin Diener, *Icon/Altar: Elements* pendant. Sterling, brass, copper, drawing by S. Barnes, carnelian, moonstone, sunstone, and other gems. 4 x 4".
Photo by Dean Powell.

switch to a burnisher or a leather polishing stick to give the setting its final finish. Once you've gone through the process a half dozen times, you'll be surprised how quickly bezels come together.

FANCY BEZELS

After you've made a few standard bezels and understand the process, turn your imagination loose. Bezels lend themselves to all sorts of variations, including pattern, shape, color and ornamentation.

Carved Edge

Make the bezel in the usual way, then use files and a saw to cut lines, scallops and other shapes into the edge. Setting proceeds as usual.

Wide Edge

Make the bezel from thick stock, either by cutting it from sheet or by planishing a section of wire. For a small stone, you'll want something around 20 gauge, a medium size stone needs a piece about 18 gauge, and the bezel for a large stone could be made of 14 or 16 gauge. The bezel will be more difficult to form and size, but the principle is the same. Setting will require a hammer and punch to move the thicker metal, but otherwise the sequence of events is identical.

down. This process could involve a dozen pushes or a hundred; it depends on the size of the stone, height of the bezel and the power of each push.

Smooth and shape the bezel. Use a fine needle file and/or a pumice wheel on the flex shaft to smooth and shape the bezel. This requires a light touch, but can make the difference between a mediocre and a stunning bezel. After putting in this much time, don't sell the gem short by hurrying through the clean-up stage.

An important note: Most gemstones can withstand the touch of a file, as long as it's not pressed too hard, but virtually anything will be scratched by silicon carbide sandpaper. Even the apparently harmless fine papers are made of the same tough stuff as coarser grits, so never use sandpapers near a stone. Never!

Now that the shape of the bezel has been made uniformly graceful,

is tight, you won't need to solder this inner bezel in position—the same action that sets the stone will also secure the supporting inner bezel.

You can achieve the same result by soldering a narrow strip or wire onto a slightly wider one in such a way that a ledge or step is created. As mentioned

Step bezel.

Secure the completed jewelry piece to a scrap of wood with hot glue (it can be warmed later with a hair dryer to release it), or ask a friend to hold it firmly in place. Use a blunt punch and a light hammer to press the bezel over, again moving alternately from one side of the bezel to the other as you go. Start with the tool at a 45° angle, raising it during later stages until, by the last planishing, the tool is almost vertical. As above, use a fine file and a pumice wheel to smooth and shape the bezel. To create a patterned bezel, follow the same directions, including the clean up procedure, then use a sharp stamp to create a texture. Any stone can withstand this process when it's done right because all the force is on the bezel, not the stone. Having said that, I recommend trying it first on a tough stone like agate, onyx or quartz.

Step Bezel

To make a shallow stone stand up tall, use a second, internal bezel to lift it above the level of the base. This can be done by making the basic bezel described above, then fitting a shorter bezel inside. If the fit

Beth Fein, *Dog Takes a Spin on Pi* ©. Sterling, 14K, diamond, Chinese writing stone. 3½ x 1 x ³/₁₆".

above, this material, called shelf or ledge bezel, can be purchased, but only in a small size. For larger stones you'll need to make your own, and of course when you are building this at the bench, you have control over the height and thickness as well. Once the stock is made, form the bezel in the usual way, omitting the base.

Tube Setting

This variation is usually used for small faceted stones, and starts with a piece of tubing whose inner diameter is smaller than the stone, but whose outer diameter is larger. Tubing can be made to suit your needs, as explained in Chapter 7. Cut a length of tubing of the desired height and solder it into place on the jewelry piece. After making certain the top edge of the tube is flat and even, use a *setting bur* to carve a notch around its inner circumference. This is called a *bearing,* and makes a place for the stone to rest. In a well-cut setting, the gem snaps into place, making the setting process easier.

Use a bezel pusher and burnisher to set the stone, following the guidelines given above. It's often possible to use round-nose pliers as an alternate setting tool. Use the base of the jaws, where the tapers

Robert Grey Kaylor, earrings. 18K, opal. 2 x ³⁄₄". *Photo by Ralph Gabriner.*

Use a file or sandpaper wrapped around a cylinder to shape the underside of a bezel wall so it conforms to the shape of a ring or bracelet. In this situation, no bottom is needed for the bezel.

are largest, to squeeze two opposite points simultaneously.

FITTING BEZELS TO CURVED SURFACES

When mounting a bezel on a ring shank or bracelet, it's necessary to file the underside of the bezel wall to match the circular contour. In these cases, the bezel won't need a sheet bottom, since it sits directly on the shank. The filing action might feel a little awkward, but perseverance will be repaid with a

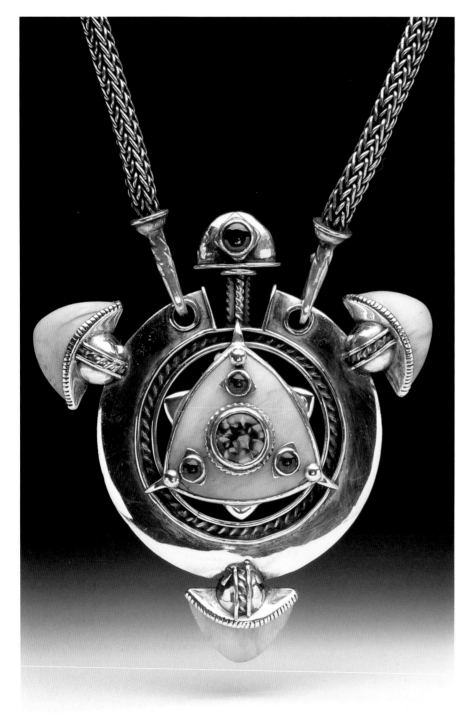

Adam Clark, pendant. Sterling, bone, amethyst, citrine. 2 x 3".

strong clean joint. Use a half-round file, or wrap sandpaper around a cylinder with a radius similar to the piece being fit. Place the bezel into position periodically to check the fit, and keep sanding until no light shows beneath the bezel. The setting can usually be balanced for soldering, but if necessary it can be tied in place with steel binding wire.

Stones can be set as usual, but of course the flat underside of the stone risks seesawing in the setting. Sprinkle a little wood sawdust into the bezel and tamp it down to make a level bed to support the stone.

Prong Settings

Prongs are no more difficult than bezels, either to construct or to set, but they require a little more precision. There are dozens of variations, not counting the ones you're about to dream up. This chapter describes a couple of the most basic styles, but first let's look at some guidelines that apply to all prong settings.

Prong Setting Guidelines

- Use strong metals.
- Prongs must be symmetrical.
- Fit is critical.

Use strong metals. Prongs do a lot of work with a small amount of metal, so the metal must be tough. Copper just isn't hard enough for prongs, and brass or sterling should be used only when the size of the stone allows a hefty gauge and broad shape. Most prong settings are made of gold, but you can practice with sterling while you develop skill and confidence.

Prongs must be symmetrical, both to look good and to properly secure a stone. Not sort-of symmetrical, but dead-on accurate. At each step of the process, examine the work from all angles to be sure it's just right.

Fit is critical. Stone setting is a breeze if the prongs are properly fitted to the stone. A proper fit refers to both the diameter and the depth of the stone (distance from table to culet), as well as the contour of the pavilion.

Get into the habit of examining each stone before determining what kind of setting it needs. Hold a stone in tweezers and examine it under magnification to become familiar with its idiosyncrasies. Pay particular attention to the girdle and the area just below it, since this is the part of the stone that touches the setting. If it is irregular, your job in setting will be more difficult.

MAKING A CROWN SETTING

This all-purpose setting is available commercially, but it's well worthwhile to make at least a couple from scratch. And of course, there are cases when the commercial version isn't exactly what you need. The example shown below uses a 5-millimeter stone and 20-gauge sterling. When working in gold, 22 gauge will provide sufficient strength.

FABRICATION PROCESS

1   Lay out the pattern for a cone by drawing the side view of the intended shape. Extend the edges, then place a compass point on that intersection and draw arcs from the top and bottom of the cone. Use the compass to step off the stone diameter three times along the larger arc, and connect this point to the original center point. Transfer this shape to sheet metal and saw it out.

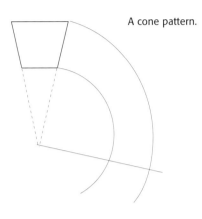

A cone pattern.

2   Bend the cone with round-nose pliers. Use a file to prepare the seam, and solder the cone closed with hard solder.

3   Make the cone round by working it with scribes, punches and dapping tools. Set the gem into position to be certain the size is accurate, and cut away excess on the top or bottom. File the bottom (the tip of the cone) flat.

4   Use a saw to carefully remove the bottom section of the cone.

5   Divide the base into four or six equal units and make a notch with a triangular file. These notches should not fall on the solder seam, which means most of the soldered area will be cut away; see step 7, below. Once the V-shapes are cut, use a file to angle them gracefully outward. The object is to preserve strength while making the setting appear delicate.

6   Reattach the base.

7   Invert the setting and use a saw to cut away the areas between the ornamental notches just made. Use small files and/or burs to make these openings uniform and graceful.

8   Finish the crown with sandpaper to make it smooth and deli-

MAKING A CROWN SETTING

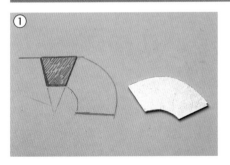

1 Template for a cone, and sheet metal piece ready to form.

2 Cut off the bottom section and file small notches around the lower part of the cone.

3 Reattach the base and saw triangles to form prongs.

4 The finished crown setting.

cate. Then solder it into position on a jewelry piece.

SETTING A STONE IN PRONGS

1 Using a rod of sticky wax to grip the stone, hold it in position in the setting to check the height. If the stone is sitting too high, the setting can be expanded a little by pressing a dapping punch into it.

2 *For round stones:* Select a setting bur that perfectly matches the diameter of the stone. If a perfect match is not available, choose a smaller bur.

   With the bur mounted in a flex shaft, hold the tool vertically and lower it into the setting with the bur turning as slowly as possible. As soon as it touches the prongs, remove the tool and check to see that the bur has made identical marks on each prong. If one is untouched, or cut deeper than the others, use pliers to move the prong to the correct angle. Cut notches that will seat the stone and aid in bending over the prong. Notches should be cut about one-third of the way through the prong

3 *For oval and other shapes:* Use a Hart bur or small spherical bur to make the following cuts.

   With the stone in position, use a felt tip pen to mark a location on each prong just below the point where the stone touches it. With the bur turning as slowly as possible, cut away about one-third of each prong at the marked location.

4 Use a small blade or a fine file to scrape the sides of each prong, removing burs formed in the last process.

5 Set the stone into place, ideally with a snap fit. Check to ensure that it is level and equally engaged in all the prongs. If not,

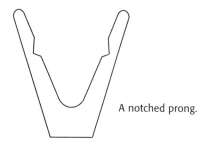

A notched prong.

use a file or bur to adjust the notches as needed to correct the problem, but go slowly so you don't cut away too much.

6 With the stone properly seated, use wire cutters to snip off each prong at the height of the table on the stone. This can be done with the stone in position if you hold it in place with your finger.

7 Remove the stone and file the tops of the prongs to make them even, then shape each one individually, usually with a slight taper.

8 Snap the stone into place and use a bezel pusher or pliers to press each prong tip inward. Press each of the prongs halfway, check the stone, then complete the setting process. Use magnification to check each prong and to ensure that the stone is level.

9 Use a ball bur or a beading tool to shape each prong. The former is a cutting tool, so go slowly. Beading tools require pressure, so again, go slowly, revolving the tool to shape and harden each prong. Use a bristle brush and white diamond on the flex shaft to polish the prongs, and you're done! (Exhale.)

PEDESTAL PRONG SETTING

This versatile, hybrid setting lends itself to cabs and faceted stones, large and small, symmetrical and irregular. It's not accurate to say it's

Sandra Zilker, *Sticks & Stones* pin series. Sterling, stones, painted wood.

Rebecca Kraemer, *Fickle Fate* necklace. Fine silver, sterling, gemstones, brass, copper. 1³/₄ x 1¹/₂".
Photo by Brett Bennett.

the only setting you'll ever need, but it's close. The first step is to make a "pedestal" that supports the stone from underneath. This can be as shallow as a millimeter or as deep as you want it. Whatever the choice, the pedestal should be shaped exactly like the footprint of the stone. Once it's made, set the stone on the pedestal and view it from directly overhead. No metal should be visible. If setting a faceted stone, use a bur or round needle file to cut a *chamfer* or bevel around the inner edge of the top side of the pedestal.

This is one of the few settings that can accommodate asymmetrical stones and odd numbers of prongs. Choose whatever configuration best secures the stone, and cut that number of prongs. Nearly any wire can be used, but with round wire, I like to file a flat facet on one side to ensure a stronger grip against the side of the pedestal. The example shown on page 83 uses a rectangular strip made by hammering a piece of 16-gauge wire. Cut prongs that are about three times the finished length, and make a point on the bottom of each one.

Clean up the outside surface of the pedestal, coat it with flux, and set it onto a soft firebrick or similar soldering surface. Gripping each prong with pliers, press it firmly into the brick so it stands in position around the pedestal. Apply small pieces of hard solder to each prong, and heat.

If a prong is tilted, grip the setting in cross-lock tweezers to secure it, reflux the piece, and heat it until the solder becomes molten. Gently grab the prong with tweezers and reposition it as necessary to ensure that it is vertical and properly spaced. This sounds harder than it is.

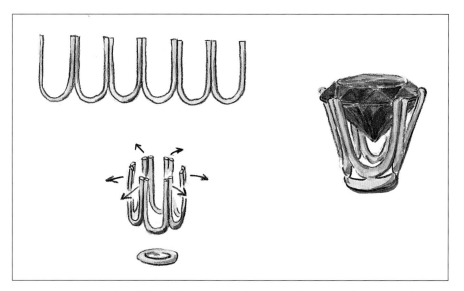

A fabricated prong setting. This simple, elegant setting starts with pieces of round wire bent to look like the letter "U." They are soldered side-by-side, then bent into a cylinder that is soldered closed. Attach a small ring to the base and bend each prong outward to create a cone shape. The prongs are then notched and the stone is set as described in the text.

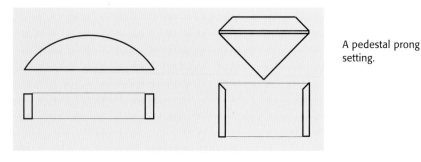

A pedestal prong setting.

When the unit is assembled and pickled, use snips to cut off the part of each prong that projected into the brick. File the underside of the setting to an attractive shape. Test the stone in position and make adjustments as necessary. If the fit is too tight, file the inner surface of the prongs with a small flat file. Check the fit frequently so you don't go too far. If the fit is a little loose, grip the pedestal with ring-forming pliers and bend a couple of the prongs inward.

With the stone in position, use wire cutters to snip off excess material. Remove the stone and file the top of each prong to guarantee a uniform height. Then shape the prongs, reinsert the stone, and press the prongs over, using a bezel pusher or pliers depending on the amount of force required. After setting, use a pumice wheel and felt buff to refine and polish each prong.

Basha Burwell,
bracelet. Sterling,
beach stones. *Photo
by Robert Diamante.*

MAKING A PEDESTAL PRONG

1 Position sharpened wire prongs around the pedestal. Press into fire brick for soldering.

2 Trim off extra length on the prongs and file the underside smooth.

3 Complete other soldering, in this case adding a decorative bail.

4 Set the stone with a bezel pusher…

5 …or with pliers, as shown.

6 The finished piece.

7

Mechanisms & Chains

P*art of the pleasure of making jewelry comes from its use as personal adornment. This brings with it several parameters, or constraints on design, such as appropriate size, weight and shape. It also means that a piece needs to function, with trustworthy hinges, secure catches, and chains with just the right amount of flexibility. For the true craftsman, these are not problems to be dodged, but challenges that energize the process.*

Pin Findings

Pin Finding Guidelines

- The clasp must hold the jewelry securely.
- Its design should be consistent with the character of the piece.
- It should be easy to latch and unlatch.
- The pin should not damage fabric.

The attachments for a pin or brooch usually consist of three elements: hinge, catch and pin stem. All can be made at the bench or purchased ready-made, and a combination of the two can be used. Pin findings should be placed near the top of the pin and as far apart as possible for maximum stability. A well-designed pin joint will hold

Michele Mercaldo, brooch. 14K, sterling. 1¼".

the pin stem slightly above the back of the brooch, so that it needs a little downward pressure to secure it in the catch.

SHAPING THE PIN STEM

The tip of the stem, the part that penetrates the wearer's clothing, should be pointed without being pointy. Instead of a thin, dangerous point that will snag fabric, shape the tip to resemble a bullet, curving to a point only for the last 3 or 4 millimeters. Use a file, rotating the wire freely, then smooth off any marks with fine sandpaper. To further polish and harden the tip, stroke it with a burnisher (the tip of your round-nose pliers will do) as if you were whittling a point on a stick. The resulting tip will find its way between threads rather than through them, and leave a garment unharmed.

PIN ENCLOSURE

This basic pin catch is versatile and secure. It encloses the tip of the pin, and lends itself to decoration to make it coordinate with the overall design. Follow the photographs on page 86 for construction information, but keep in mind that the simple box can be stamped, pierced or shaped.

PIN JOINTS

A good pin joint should allow the pin stem to open fully, stop at the correct height to create tension in the catch, and adjust easily when the tolerances begin to wear out. Commercially made pin joints are quick to apply, reliable and efficient, but sometimes a design calls for a unique arrangement. Attention given to a rarely seen detail like this is sometimes what distinguishes a really special piece.

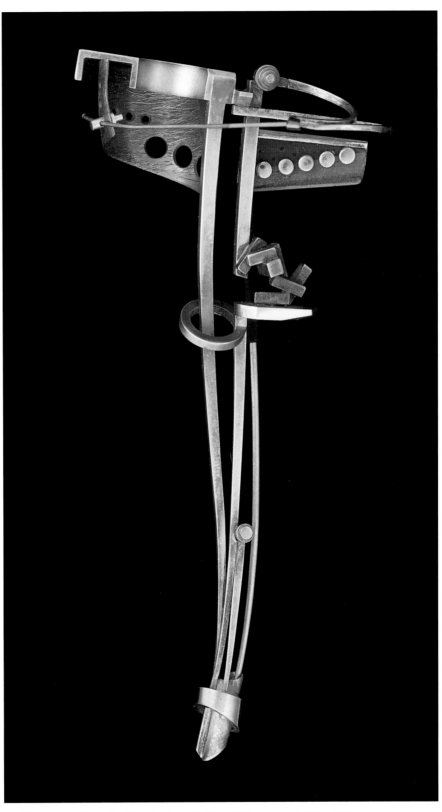

David Peterson, fibula. Sterling, titanium, niobium, 14K, parcel gilt. 3½ x 1½".

Pendants

The word *pendant* is derived from the Latin word for hanging down, and describes an ornament that is suspended from a cord or chain. Though it's a fine distinction, this is different from a necklace in the relative importance of the hanging element to the cord or chain that supports it. In the case of a pendant, decisions about size, color, finish and detail of the cord or chain are determined by what will best complement the pendant. In the case of a necklace, the whole unit is conceived as being of equal importance.

In many cases the best option for a pendant is a machine-made chain, which can be bought finished in several popular lengths or by the inch. You get what you pay for in chains, so avoid the super-low-price models; they are made of extremely thin metal and tend to kink and break easily. Remember that commercial chain can be patinated, which is sometimes useful

Jan Baum, *Structure* pendant/locket. Nickel silver, bronze, plated chain. 2⅞ x 1¼ x ⅝". ©1996. The closed piece is shown at right.
Photo by Phil Harris.

MAKING A BASIC CATCH

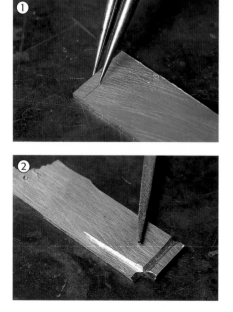

1 Use dividers to mark off lines parallel to the edge.

2 Use a needle file to cut two deep grooves.

3 Reinforce the bends and corners with solder.

4 The catch and pin joint are soldered onto the back of a brooch.

5 The assembled pin finding.

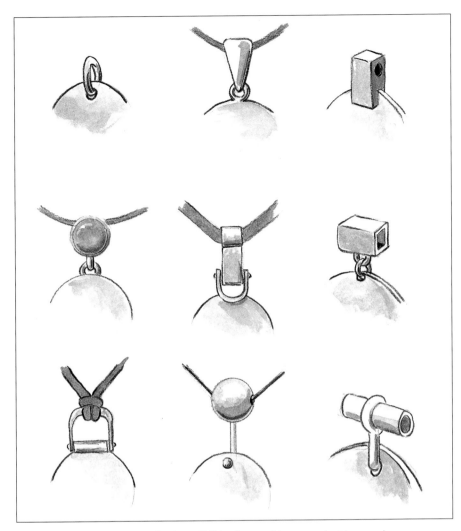

Here are a few of the thousands of possibilities for attaching a pendant to a cord.

Joana Kao, *I Never Liked Musical Chairs.*
Sterling, 24K. 2³⁄₄ x 1³⁄₄".
Photo by Doug Yaple.

CLASPS

What could be more frustrating than having a beautiful piece of jewelry you are afraid to wear because you don't trust the clasp? It's important—both functionally and visually—that clasps be secure. Many fine machine-made clasps are available, and in many cases they are the best choice. Don't skimp on quality, and remember that you can alter a commercial clasp to make it best meet your specific needs.

Even with the many good commercial options available, there are still situations that call for a bench-

in making the chain relate to your handmade pendant. Similarly, a handmade clasp can enhance an otherwise commonplace chain.

BAILS

The *bail* connects a pendant to the chain that supports it. It can be as simple as a jump ring or as fancy as your imagination can dream up; the decision should be dictated by the pendant design and the overall effect you are trying to achieve. Include the bail in your design from the very beginning, keeping the following general rules in mind.

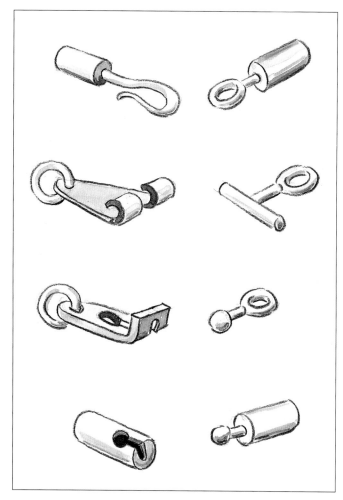

A good clasp is secure, easy to operate, and in harmony with the rest of the piece.

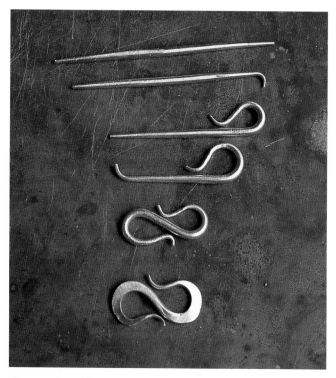

The steps in making an S-hook.

made alternative, and there's nothing like the snap of a well-fitted clasp to boost your confidence as a jeweler. These general guidelines apply to all clasps.

Clasp Guidelines

- They must be secure.
- They must be manageable, even at the back of the neck.
- They should harmonize with the rest of the piece.
- They should have a mechanism to allow tightening when they loosen through wear.
- They should be made of a durable metal—usually sterling or gold.

S-Hook

This is about as basic as it gets—easy to make, secure, attractive and relatively easy to operate. The key to a graceful shape lies in making a smooth taper; the strength comes from planishing the curve.

1 For a medium-size hook, cut a piece of 16-gauge round wire 1¹/₂" (40 mm) long.
2 File a taper from the center toward each end; smooth with sandpaper
3 Bend one tip into a tiny half circle, then bend that half of the wire into a loop that curves in the opposite direction.
4 Make a small half-circle bend in

the other tip, placing it on the same side as the large loop.
5 Bend a second large loop, again reversing the direction of the curl at the tip.
6 Use a polished hammer to planish the apex of the two large curves slightly. This makes the cross section in these areas rectangular, which, in turn, makes the curve rigid.
7 Adjust the gap at each end to be slightly smaller than the ring that will go into the hook. The ring should snap into place, and resist coming out without some effort.

T-Bar

This is another classic, and lends itself especially to bracelets. The two elements are nothing more than a straight rod and a loop; these can be miniature or massive depending on the needs of the

piece, and can be made from any sort of wire.

Start by cutting a rod and attaching a small jump ring at its midpoint. The chain is connected to the jump ring so that the bar can pivot to the point where it falls parallel to the chain. In this position it can be easily fed through a loop on the other end of the chain. Once through, the bar falls to a perpendicular position and secures the closure.

LEFT: AutumnDawnGriffiths, chains. Sterling, stone beads. *Photo by Dean Powell, Newton, MA.*

BELOW: Christopher Hentz, *Aura* necklace. Sterling, hand-wrapped cables in fine silver. 20 x 1½" diameter. *Photo by Ralph Gabriner.*

The lengths of various elements of a T-bar are critical, but not difficult to understand or correct. The bar, with its small loop, must pass through the large loop freely. The length of the bar must be such that even when slid all the way to one side of the large loop, it cannot come back through. The best bet is to start oversized and trim the bar as needed.

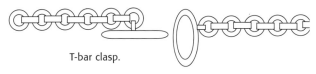

T-bar clasp.

Chains

There's something almost magical about making a flexible, slinky thing like a chain from a rigid material like metal. Chains are one of those delightful parts of jewelry making that can challenge and reward a person at every stage of development. In addition, chain making offers rich opportunity for soldering practice and teaches the value of working methodically.

Chains are often worn by themselves, and of course are used to carry charms, watches and pendants. Just as a frame should complement but not dominate a painting, a chain should be neither so bland that it lessens the other components, nor so fancy that it overpowers them. I find it helpful to have a collection of chains around to test with a pendant. Broken or base-metal chains will suffice and can be found at discount stores and flea markets.

In the same way that a painting looks funny if hung too high or too low on the wall, the length of a chain should be carefully chosen to show the pendant to best advantage. The longer the chain, the deeper the angle of the "V" made by the chain on the wearer. This angle is part of the appearance of

the piece, and should coordinate with the lines of the pendant.

MAKING JUMP RINGS

Jump rings are small circles of wire. They have dozens of uses, among them "jumping" the gap between parts, as for instance when a charm is attached to a bracelet chain. Because it's usually easier to make a few rings than a single one, make extras and set them aside for future use. Always open jump rings by twisting them front-to-back rather than by spreading them open; a spread ring will never return to a perfect circle.

If you're using wire that is curled or kinked, start by making it really straight. Clamp one end in a bench vise and grab the other end

with a heavy pair of pliers that will get a solid grip. Pull the wire straight outward, away from the vise, until you feel it stretch. The effect is usually dramatic.

To make rings, wrap the straightened wire around a mandrel of the appropriate diameter. A mandrel is nothing more than a rod of dense material; nails, spikes, knitting needles, welding rods and similar found objects are all useful as jump-ring mandrels. A graduated collection of drill bits can also come in handy—wrap the wire around the solid shaft, not the grooved, cutting end of the bit.

And what is the "appropriate" diameter? When making chain, guess at the size links you think would look good, and start there. Because it's not a science, I usually make up a few inches of chain—maybe 20 to 30 links—in copper or brass to test a size without incurring the cost of precious metal.

Make a tidy coil by wrapping the wire around the rod, taking pains to lay each wire snugly

When making jump rings, wind the wire tightly to ensure uniform loop size.

against the previous loop. To speed things up when you're making hundreds of loops, you can secure the rod in a variable speed hand drill, but be careful to run the drill at the slowest possible speed. Do not use a drill press, which doesn't offer the sensitive speed control you'll need.

Rings made of fine wire, say, under 24 gauge, can be cut with scissors; other jump rings should be cut from the coil with the jeweler's saw. Use a fine blade, mounted in the usual way, and work over a sweeps drawer or with a towel spread across your lap to catch the rings as they fall. Some people slide the coil off the mandrel and hold it in their fingers while cutting, while others prefer to cut on the mandrel, sliding the coil off the end as each ring is cut. Either way, angle the blade so that a groove is cut into the second loop before the first loop is cut through. In this way the blade is always securely tracked and the task moves ahead quickly.

An alternate method uses a thin disk of silicon carbide called a *separating disk*. This wafer of abrasive is mounted on a mandrel and put in the flexible shaft. Wear goggles and use the tool to cut a line along the coiled wire.

The best way to make oval rings is to create and solder the rings as circles, then stretch each link on a pair of round-nose pliers after the chain is assembled. In cases where the links are not going to be soldered, it's possible to tape two round mandrels together and wrap the wire around that. You'll find that the wire grabs onto the mandrel, so you'll have to work a bit to pull it off. A separating disk is especially recommended for this situation because it cuts the links without needing to have the coil removed from the mandrel.

Joana Kao, *Search* brooch. Sterling, 18K. 4³/₄ x 1". *Photo by Doug Yaple.*

CONSTRUCTING A BASIC CHAIN

The most basic family of chains, called *cable chains*, consists of a series of rings, each passing through its immediate neighbor. This is the kind of basic chain you might make with strips of paper to hang on a Christmas tree. Because size, shape, material, and surface are all variable, the possibilities are literally endless. Imagine, you could make a chain a day for the rest of your life and still have no two alike!

The most efficient way to assemble a cable chain involves a systematic sequence that combines increasingly larger sub-units, as described below.

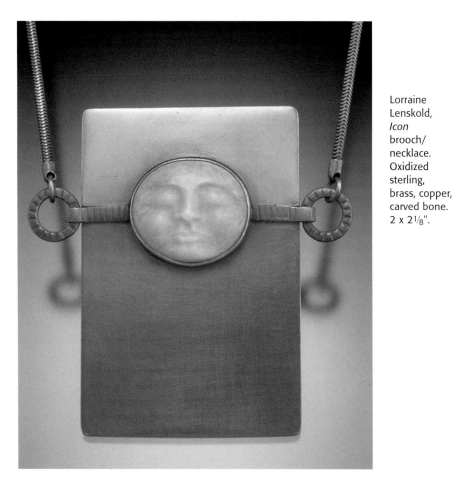

Lorraine Lenskold, *Icon* brooch/ necklace. Oxidized sterling, brass, copper, carved bone. 2 x 2⅛".

Constructing a Basic Chain

1 Wrap a wire around a mandrel and cut links. A lot of links.

2 Close half of the links and set them aside in a separate pile.

3 Solder each of the remaining links, preferably with hard solder. Make each link a separate, closed loop.

4 Slide two of the soldered links onto one of the open ones. Close it and lay it on the soldering block so the joint is exposed. Do this with all the soldered links, then solder the exposed joints.

5 Slide two of these groups of three onto one of the remaining open loops. Close it and set it on the soldering block. Repeat until all the three-groups have become incorporated into groups of seven.

6 Continue this way until all the links have been used. When all soldering is completed, pickle the chain to clean it.

7 After soldering, the links can be manipulated by bending, hammering, stamping and coloring.

MAKING A LOOP-IN-LOOP CHAIN

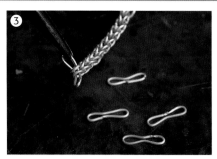

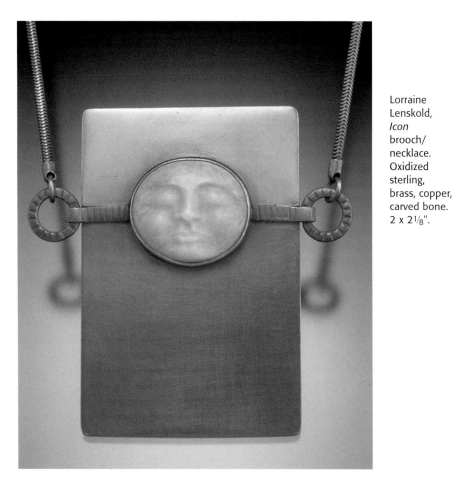

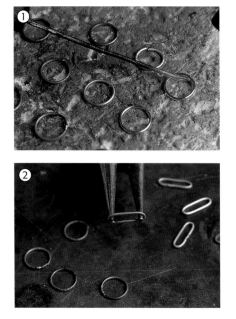

1 Pick-solder with tiny chips to close links.

2 Stretch each link into a long oval.

3 Pinch the links and feed each one through the next.

4 Some links will need to be stretched to allow the next link to pass through.

5 Press each link onto a scribe to refine the shape and make the chain more flexible.

Finishing of chains—this one and every other—must only be done by hand. Polishing chains on a machine risks serious damage to both you and the chain!

LOOP-IN-LOOP CHAIN

This beautiful chain is also called Roman, Etruscan, sailors' or money chain. It's flexible and versatile, and can be made in dense or open variations. Even the most basic version offers a wealth of options by simply changing the size of the wire and the loop. The distinguishing feature of all these variations is the building block of a soldered or fused long oval link. These are prepared as individual units, from which the chain is assembled with no further soldering needed.

Constructing Loop-in-Loop Chain

1 Make jump rings as described above. With loop-in-loop chain, it's especially important to start with a couple of dozen links to be sure you have the wire and loop size you want. Almost any combination will make a workable chain; consult the chart on page 94 for examples of wire-loop relationships.

2 Links can be fused or soldered; either way, the goal is to avoid a lump at the seam. Fusing is fastest, and fairly easy with fine silver or high-karat gold, but for sterling, I use tiny bits of hard solder. How tiny? I roll the solder as thin as the rolling mill will go, then double the sheet and roll it again. Then I cut the smallest pieces possible. Really tiny! Use a needle tool as a pick when soldering.

3 Stretch the rings on round-nose pliers by tugging the plier handles open.

4 Bend one of the loops in half and secure it on a twist of wire that will act as a handle until

style	18 gauge	20 gauge	22 gauge	24 gauge
Single	2/32" (9.5)	10/32" (7.9)	8/32" (6.3)	6/32" (4.7)
Pinched	20/32" (16)	13/32" (10.3)	13/32" (10.3)	8/32" (6.3)
Double	12/32" (9.5)	10/32" (7.9)	8/32" (6.3)	6/32" (4.7)

Recommended Wire and Mandrel Sizes for Loop-in-Loop Links [inches (mm)]

(From *Classical Loop-in-Loop Chains* by J.R. Stark and J.R. Smith. Used with permission.)

Rebecca Reimers Cristol, *Nurture V: Ovum.* Oxidized sterling and fine silver, 18K, 22K, handcarved Chinese turquoise. 1¹/₁₆ x 1¹/₄".

the chain is long enough to be easily held. Feed a loop through the two "wickets" at the top of the chain. Fold this new loop in half to create two new wickets, through which the next loop is passed. Continue in this way until the chain is complete.

Some people like to bend all the loops into the V shape as a separate step, then feed these into place. Try both methods to see which you prefer. The end results are identical.

5 Anneal the chain, then refine the shape of each link by pressing it over a scribe. Set a polished, tapered scribe point vertically in a vise and slide each link down on it as shown, rotating the link and pressing it down four times. This will make more sense when you have the chain in your hand—you'll see that each link has, in effect, four sides. The process goes faster than you might think, and has dramatic results as it turns a lumpy stiff chain into a smoothly articulate marvel.

Note: Don't leave the scribe unattended, even for a minute. If you are not actively using it, remove it from the vise so no one gets hurt.

LOOP-IN-LOOP VARIATIONS

There are many beautiful variations of loop-in-loop chain. For our purposes here I'll only hint at what can be done, with a nod to chain addicts to explore on their own. In every case these variations start with the long oval links described above.

Pinched Loop (Sailor's Knot)

Shape the links into a "barbell" by using flat-nose pliers and round-nose pliers at the same time. Hold the loop in the opened round pliers, then squeeze the midsection

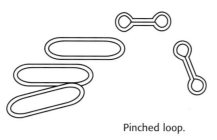
Pinched loop.

with the flats. Lightly planish the rounded ends of each loop, then assemble the chain as usual.

Double Loop-in-Loop

Start by putting one loop through another as you would to start the basic loop-in-loop chain described above. Press the two loops together so their "mid-sections" are compressed. Use a scribe to open a passage here (arrow), through which the third loop will be inserted. It might be helpful to attach a short

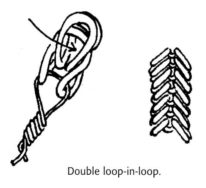
Double loop-in-loop.

twist of wire to the bottom to serve as a handle until the chain is long enough to provide a suitable grip.

Continue threading loops, one after the next, always passing through a "double" wicket. The result is a more complex-looking chain, with a distinct herringbone pattern.

Two-Way Single Loop-in-Loop

Solder two links together in the form of a "+" and solder on a handle of some sort for easier gripping—it can be sawn off and cleaned later. Curl up the ends of both loops to form a basket shape

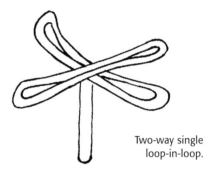
Two-way single loop-in-loop.

and drive a new loop (#3) through the wickets of the lower loop. Rotate the assembly and insert a loop (#4) through the wickets of what is *now* the lower of the two available wickets. Continue in this way until you're done.

Examples of Link-to-Chain Proportions for Single Loop-in-Loop

wire (B&S)	loop inside diameter	chain diameter	links per inch
22	10 mm	5 mm	13
24	7 mm	4 mm	18
26	6 mm	3.5 mm	20
28	5 mm	3 mm	24

This chain, in effect, weaves two basic chains together, one inside the other. Unlike the chains mentioned above, the proportions of this variation are important. If the loops are too large or the wire too small the result can look distorted, even if the craftsmanship is flawless. Use the suggestions from the chart on page 94 to get started, then do some tests of your own.

The two-way single loop-in-loop works nicely with mixed colors. If you make links of two metals, say, silver and gold, you can either alternate every pair (gold, gold, silver, silver, gold, gold), which gives a sort of checkered effect, or alternate every loop (gold, silver, gold, silver, gold) which make a square chain with two gold faces and two silver faces.

WOVEN CHAIN

This textile-like chain is not made of links, but created by threading a single wire back and forth on itself. Though it resembles spool weaving, it's not quite the same. As with the other chains mentioned so far, it presents a wide range of possibilities. The tools are simple, and because no soldering is needed, this is a technique you can do as easily on the living room couch as in the studio.

You'll need a pair of chain-nose pliers, wire cutters and a scribe or other tapered point. If you don't have a point, a suitable tool can be made by grinding or filing a taper on the last two inches of a 5-inch piece of coat hanger or similar wire. I suggest wrapping the wire with tape to make a comfortable handle.

Woven Chain Guidelines

- Try to keep the loops the same size.
- Use pliers to pull the wire. Using your fingers will stress the wire and cause it to harden and break.
- Smaller loops are easier to work with than large loops, especially when getting started.
- Use each loop only once.

Constructing Woven Chain

1 Starting with a two-foot length of wire, bend a series of up and down arcs that looks like the photo. The goal in this example is to have three "peaks" and two "valleys," each about an inch tall. One end of the wire should be short, no more than two inches.

2 Squeeze the wire together and wrap the short end around it until it is used up. The result will look like a hank of rope.

3 Pull the three loops at the top (the "peaks" in step 1) into a radially symmetrical pattern. In other words, twist them until the three loops lean outward from a central point. They will resemble the pistil of a flower.

4 Take up the long wire and feed it through any one of the loops, *going from the inside to the outside.* Pull it up snugly so no additional loop is made.

At this point you should have a structure of three loops with a wire projecting out from one

CONSTRUCTING A WOVEN CHAIN

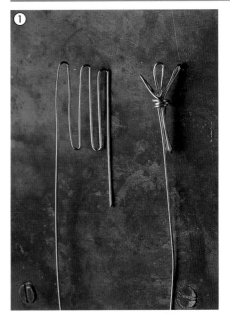

1 The chain starts with bends pulled into a wrapped bunch.

2 Feed the wire back into the loop it comes out of, then out through an adjacent loop.

3 Use a tight twist to splice in a new section of wire. Trim to about half the size shown.

4 Roll the chain over a wooden cylinder to make it more flexible.

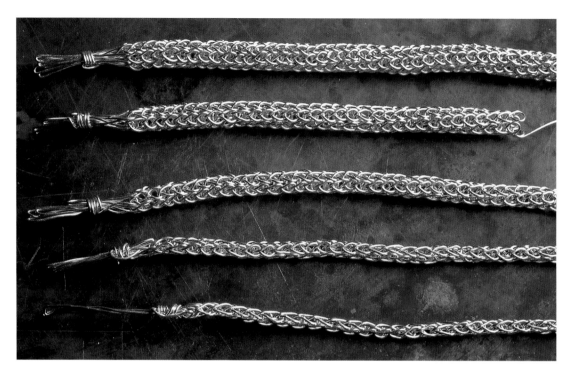

Samples of 3-, 4-, 5-, 6- and 7-loop chains, in this case all made with 26-gauge wire.

loop. This is home base; from now on your structure should always have *three loops with a wire leaving*.

5 Feed the end of the wire back into the loop it is coming out of, and go out through one of the other loops. Pull the wire to take up some of the slack, then set the tip of your scribe in the loop and pull the wire tight onto it. Notice that if the scribe were not there, the loop would be pulled through and would disappear. It doesn't matter whether the chain grows clockwise or counterclockwise, but once you get started you'll need to be consistent.

6 Before removing the scribe from the newly formed loop, lift the scribe so it levers the loop into a "standing" position. Rotate the chain in your fingers so the loop with the wire leaving is facing you and repeat steps 4, 5, and 6. The chain grows spirally, each loop being used once and giving rise to a new loop that projects out from it.

7 When the original two feet of wire is almost used up, it's time to add another length. With the last inch or so, make a half stitch—that is, go into the loop from which the wire projects, but do not continue on out the adjacent loop. Instead, feed the end of a two-foot piece of wire into the adjacent loop and twist it together with the remaining bit of the original wire. Use pliers to make the connection tight, then snip off the excess, leaving no more than a quarter inch of twist. You are now back on track: *three loops with a wire leaving*. Continue weaving as before, taking pains that the twist stays safely tucked into the core of the chain.

As a rule of thumb, a foot of wire equals an inch of woven chain, though this is very approximate and depends on the size of the loops, the diameter of the wire, and the tightness of the weave.

Finishing the Chain

This chain doesn't unravel, so you don't need to tie it off when done. Just stop weaving and that's that. This also means you can cut off the starting section, not only the handle area from steps 1-3 above, but also the "practice" section you may have made before finding your rhythm.

The chain can be pulled lightly through a drawplate to make it more even. If you don't have one, a simple drawplate can be made by drilling a series of holes of decreasing size in a small, flat piece of hardwood. You can also roll the chain on a table top under a piece of wood. Either way, follow that step by annealing. To avoid uneven heating, lay the chain on the solder block so it doesn't overlap itself.

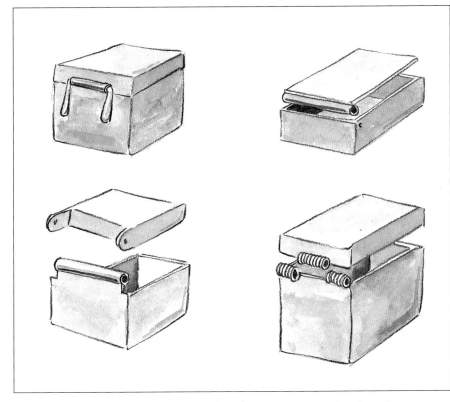

Hinge variations. The idea of a hinge is simple and open to many creative alternatives.

you won't be able to pull a tapered chain through a drawplate, so take care to keep the weaving symmetrical as you go.

Hinges

Hinges have scores of uses in jewelry, from lockets to bracelets to poison rings. They allow an otherwise oversized piece to flex with the body, and can add excitement and mystery to a design. The possibilities are vast.

Hinge Guidelines

- Prepare a precise seat for the tubing; time spent here will always be rewarded.
- Be certain every surface is clean before soldering.
- Trim all edges to remove burs, even the tiniest ones.
- Do not overheat a joint—remove the torch as soon as the solder starts to flow.
- Confidence is a valuable ally.

MAKING TUBES

Hinges consist of *knuckles*—sections of tubing that are joined alternately to the two halves being hinged—and hinge pins. Knuckles

Grip a wooden dowel or hammer handle in a vise and, wrapping the chain around it loosely, stroke it back and forth to flex the weave. After a few minutes of this, anneal one more time and you're done.

Woven Chain Variations

The chain just described uses the minimum number of loops, but any additional number can be used. To make a four-loop chain, simply make four "peaks" in step one. Or make five, or six or more. The more loops you have, the larger the hollow core in the center, and of course the larger the chain itself. The chain can be made of almost any size wire, though I rarely go larger than 22 gauge and usually prefer something around 26. Alternate metals can be spliced in to create a banded chain.

To make a tapered woven structure, add loops as the chain grows.

For instance, after starting with a 3-loop chain, add a loop by simply creating one with the wire. Weave this 4-loop chain for several stitches, then add another, and so on. To reduce the taper, skip a loop periodically, folding it into the center of the chain. Of course,

A woven taper. Additional loops are added as the chain grows to create an expanding form. This example was made by Mark Leahy.

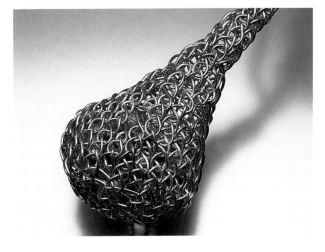

Tube Blank Sizes			
inside diameter	gauge of sheet (B&S)		
	24	26	28
3mm	11mm	10.7mm	10.5mm
4mm	14	13.8	13.6
5mm	17.3	17	16.7
6mm	20.5	20	19.9

Sara Shepherd, *This Book's Cover* brooch. Sterling, 14K. 1½ x 1¼".
Photo by Douglas Yaple.

are usually all the same size and traditionally appear in odd numbers, usually three or five. They are typically made of tubing, but you can also make a coil of wire (as for jump rings), flood it with solder, and cut off sections to be used for a hinge.

Sterling and gold tubing can be purchased from any company that supplies precious metal, while copper and brass tubes are often sold in hobby and craft stores. The range of sizes might be limited, but you can reduce tubing to a desired size with a drawplate. There are also times when it's handy to know how to make your own tubing, for instance when using an unusual metal or a size that is not commercially available.

Tube Making Process

1 Roll or planish a strip of sheet metal until very thin, somewhere around 26 gauge or finer.

2 Cut and file a straight edge, then use dividers to drag out a parallel line. The width of this strip should be a little more than three times the intended inside diameter of the tube. For

MAKING A TUBE

1 The tubing blank is prepared with smooth, parallel edges.

2 Begin the form by tapping the blank into a wooden groove.

3 Draw the tube through the drawplate; keep the motion perpendicular to the plate.

4 Solder the tube seam with hard solder.

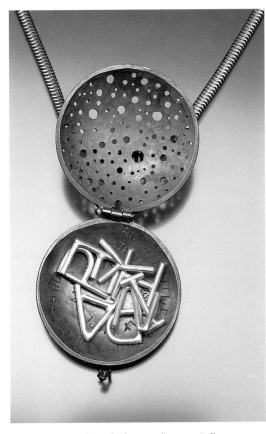

j.e. Paterak, *Epiphany* locket. Sterling. 1¾" diameter.

a 3-millimeter tube, for instance, make a strip that is 10 or 11 millimeters wide. Cut neatly, and file the edges so they are true. Cut a point on one end to allow the strip to be inserted through a hole in the drawplate.

3 Form the strip into a channel by striking a metal rod set on the strip as it lays in a wooden groove. Neither the groove nor the rod need be exactly the size of the final tube, as long as they are of a similar scale. Use pliers to ensure that the metal curls at least three-quarters of the way around the rod, paying special attention to the pointed end of the strip.

4 Pull the tube through a drawplate, keeping it perpendicular to the plate. Move from larger to smaller holes until the seam closes. Anneal if necessary; it usually isn't.

As soon as the edges touch, stop drawing, and solder the seam, using solder chips placed at half-inch intervals.

5 After soldering and pickling, the tube can be drawn down further if desired. This will not only reduce the diameter, but thicken the tube wall, as well.

MAKING A STANDARD HINGE

1 Prepare the seat by first filing an estimated 45° angle on each surface. When laid beside each other, the two pieces will form a V-groove for the tubing. Hold the two pieces together and use a round file to convert this straight-sided groove into a curved *bearing* that matches the contour of the tubing.

Anastacia Pesce, *Decision* locket. Sterling, fine silver, 18K, 22K, pearl, tourmaline. 3¼ x 1⅛".

MAKING A STANDARD HINGE

1 File the edges of the pieces at an angle; when laid together they should form a "V."

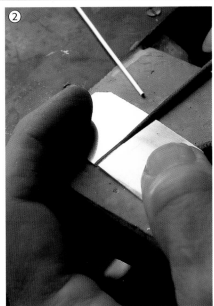

2 Use a round needle file to give the groove a rounded contour matching the knuckles.

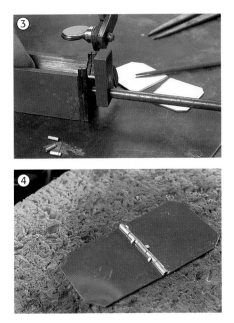

3-4 Use a tube-cutting jig to ensure straight edges and uniform size. Set a small piece of solder onto each knuckle.

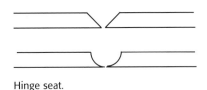

5 The ends of the hinge pin are lightly riveted to secure it in place.

2 Clean finger oils off the tubing with Scotch-Brite while the tube is long and easy to hold on to, then cut off the intended number of knuckles.

Because tubing cut freehand tends to have an angled end, use a jig to help hold the saw blade vertical. Examine each knuckle after sawing and remove any burs that might cling to the ends.

Hinge seat.

3 Flux both sides of the workpiece and set the tubes into place so they touch each other. Now you can see the importance of proper filing: if the groove is exactly the size of the tube, the knuckles will go just where you want them to.

4 Place a small piece of solder on each knuckle so it bridges the piece and the tubing. Heat one side until the solder flows, then heat the other side. In both cases, remove the torch as soon as the solder starts to move.

5 After pickling, slide a snug fitting wire into the tubes, checking each side independently to confirm alignment before attempting a complete assembly. If a lot of work is still needed, you might want to leave a piece of base metal wire in place to protect the tubes from being accidentally squashed.

6 Make the final assembly only after all soldering is done, all stones are set, and any patina is complete. A light riveting action on the ends of the hinge pin will hold it in place.

⑧ Casting

Casting is a significantly different approach to jewelry making—one in which the principal design work is done not in metal, but in a softer, more easily shaped material such as wax. Typically, from this "pattern" a mold is made that has the exact shapes, textures and dimensions of the intended object—in reverse. Molten metal is then forced into the mold, where it assumes the contours and surface of the original object. The process called "direct casting" is a bit different, and we'll cover it first.

Direct Casting Methods

When the earliest metalsmiths refined their material from ore, they realized that it took the shape of the gouge in the ground into which it was poured. It was a short step from that realization to the idea of pouring not just a crude ingot, but a shape that closely resembled the intended form.

In that tradition, the first form of direct casting is to make an ingot (a process illustrated in the appendix). Scraps of metal are melted and poured into a flat-walled vessel called an *ingot mold*. The resulting piece can be thinned, smoothed and otherwise shaped to create stock for fabrication. Though not an essential skill for a jeweler,

Joana Kao, *Keep in Touch* pin. Sterling, 18K, bronze. 2¾ x 1¾". *Photo by Richard Nicol.*

making ingots offers the double advantage of reusing scraps while at the same time providing a fuller understanding of our material.

To create a mold that takes a shape other than a simple geometric ingot, you'll want a material that is soft enough to be cut or pressed to a desired shape, yet sufficiently heat-resistant to hold its form for at least a few seconds while the metal solidifies. Several materials fulfill these needs and have been used by various cultures over the centuries. The most common are clay, sand, soft stone (tufa), and the skeleton of a marine animal called a *cuttlefish*. Each of these materials deserves experimentation, and each has unique advantages. We'll focus here on direct casting into cuttlefish.

CUTTLEFISH

Small cuttlefish can be purchased from a pet store (they're used in parakeet cages) and larger pieces are available from jewelry suppliers for about a dollar apiece. You'll need a *pouring crucible*, a little *casting flux* (such as powdered borax), and a torch capable of melting the metal you intend to use. The mold is held upright in a dish of sand.

The Cuttlefish Casting Process

1 For this example, I'll use a single bone, cutting it in half to make the two parts of the mold. For a larger jewelry piece, use two cuttlefish. With a hacksaw

MAKING A CUTTLEFISH CASTING

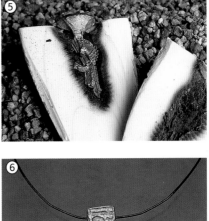

1 Cut off the tips and divide the bone into two equal sections.

2 Rub each section on sandpaper to make the bone perfectly flat.

3 Shape by compressing or scraping the bone away. The funnel shape is also hollowed out.

4 Tie the pieces together, melt the metal in a pouring crucible, and pour it into the mold.

5 The mold can be opened right away to reveal the result.

6 The finished cuttlefish casting.

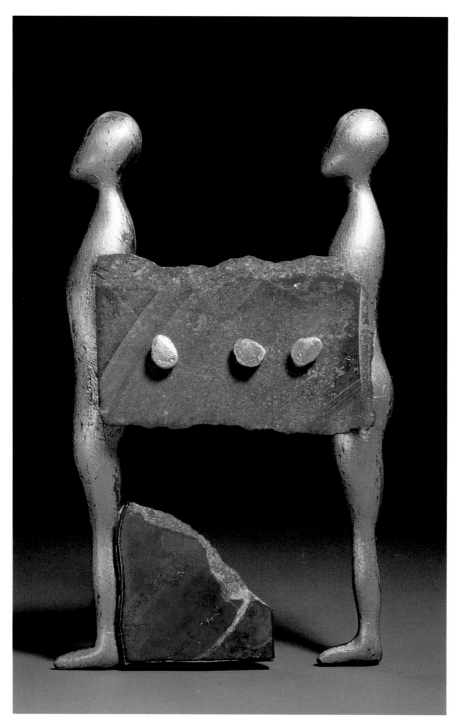

Jung-Hoo Kim, *The Connection 1* brooch. Sterling, lapis lazuli, 24K foil. 3¼ x 2".

or jeweler's saw, square off the tips and cut the bone in half. You'll see that the bone is a very soft, porous material with a plastic-like layer on one side.

2 Rub each half of the bone on a piece of coarse sandpaper to make it flat. You'll make a mess, so have a wastebasket nearby. Make the two surfaces so flat that when held together no light can be seen between them.

3 Working about an inch from the broad end of the mold, create the negative of the shape you want: where you want a projection in metal, make a depression in the mold. Particles can be compacted into the bone or scraped away; in either case, you can use very basic tools like nails, toothpicks and twigs. If you want to exaggerate the wood-grain texture of the bone, use a soft, dry paint brush to remove additional material from between the harder ridges.

4 Carve or press a channel to create an entrance for the molten metal. This is called a *sprue*, or *gate*, and it must be at least as thick as the thickest section of the object being cast. Enlarge this into a funnel opening at the top of the mold.

5 This is a one-shot technique, so look carefully to be sure you like what you've carved and are certain no constricted areas will stop the flow of metal through the mold. Set the mold halves together and check the sprue passage to be sure it's large enough to allow the metal to flow in. Err on the side of caution here, making the sprue at least an eighth inch in diameter. Bind the pieces together with wire or heavy tape and set the mold vertically into a dish of sand or pumice pebbles.

6 If this is the first time the crucible is being used, first heat it

Martha Williford Avrett, *An die Musik #1* pendant. Sterling, glass, mica, found objects, cast elements, photo. 3 x 2¾".

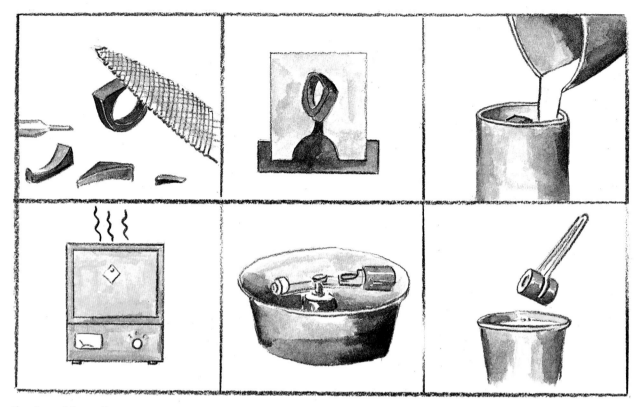

The steps of the casting process.

with a torch and sprinkle a quarter teaspoon of borax into the bowl. This creates a glassy coating that keeps the metal from sticking. Place metal into the pouring crucible, guessing generously at the amount so you won't run short. Use a torch to heat the metal until it forms a rounded blob (it should look like mercury). Add a pinch of flux midway in the melting process to protect the metal from oxides. Keep the torch on the molten mass continuously while making the pour.

7 Hold the crucible just above the cuttlefish, tilted and poised on the lip of the dish, ready to go. When the metal spins and vibrates, pour it into the mold with a smooth even motion— don't throw it, but don't stop midway, either. You will be re-warded with the foul smell of burning bone.

8 Allow the metal to cool for a minute or so, then cut the wire or tape to open the mold. Use tweezers to lift the hot piece from the mold. Remember that this is solid metal, and can be hammered, filed and soldered like any other piece.

Lost Wax Casting

By far the most common form of casting in contemporary jewelry making is *lost wax waste mold centrifugal casting*. It's a long name, but worth understanding because it tells us a lot about the process. The word *wax* tells us the model, or replica, is made of wax, while *lost* refers to the fact that the model will disappear somewhere along the way. Each model can be used just once.

The *waste mold* part of the name tells us this is true of the mold as well—it too must be destroyed (or "wasted") to retrieve the casting. Like the model, this mold can be used only once.

We know from the section on fusing that some metals, including silver and gold, will draw up into a sphere when heated. This explains why gravity alone is not sufficient to fill a large, detailed mold. And here the word *centrifugal* tells us what kind of force is used to push the molten metal into the cavity. Lost wax. Waste mold. Centrifugal casting. Got it?

OVERVIEW

Lost wax casting is not difficult, but it involves a lot of steps and can seem overwhelming at first. Each of the following procedures is described at length later on, but let's first see how they work together, and pick up some casting vocabulary as we go.

Model making

An exact model of the intended piece is made, usually in wax.

Spruing

Wax rods are attached to the model to create passageways that will lead metal into the mold cavity.

Mounting

The sprued model is secured on a rubber base that positions it in the *flask*, a short stainless steel tube.

Investing

After the flask is pressed onto the base, a plaster-like material called *investment* is mixed, freed of bubbles, and poured over the model to encase it in what we can now call the *mold*.

Burnout

After several hours drying, the mold is heated to a high temperature. The mold is cured (hardened) and the wax model burns away, leaving the cavity and sprue channels open.

Throwing

The hot mold is mounted into a spring-driven machine, where a ceramic crucible is used to contain the metal for casting. The metal is melted with a torch, the mechanism is tripped, and the casting machine whirls forcefully, slinging the molten metal into the mold.

Quench

After a few minutes of cooling down, the flask and mold are plunged into a bucket of water, in which the hot investment breaks apart and frees the casting. The

Linda Hesh, *Head for News* earrings. Sterling. 1⅝ x ⅞ x ⅝". *Photo by Ralph Gabriner.*

sprues are then cut away, the casting is cleaned up with files and sandpaper, and the final steps are taken to complete the piece.

WAXES AND MODEL MAKING

Any kind of wax can be used to make models, but most people prefer to use the highly refined, color-enhanced materials made specifically for this purpose. These fall into two families: soft and hard, or *modeling* and *carving*. The former is sold in sheet and wire, like metal, while carving waxes are sold in hollow cylinders and solid blocks.

Tools for wax working include coarse, open-toothed files and burs for hard wax, and delicate needles and dental tools for modeling wax. The latter tools are heated in the flame of a small alcohol lamp, and, when touched to the wax, cause it

to melt locally and flow together. An electric pen with a heat control is also useful for working soft wax, but not necessary unless you intend to make wax modeling a large part of your work.

Model making is the most creative part of casting, and the element that deserves your highest attention. Other steps must be done *right*, but this must be done *well*. Failure to master the technical aspects described below may result in a spoiled casting and great disappointment, but with care you can correct technical mistakes. However, even masterful casting of a mediocre model will yield only a mediocre object.

On the bright side, wax is cheap and fun to play with, so make a lot of models, free from the notion that they must all be cast. Learn to manipulate the wax, pay attention

Darrien S. Segal, *Mangrove Series* flower pendants. Sterling. 1 x 7/8". *Photo by Mark Johnston.*

MAKING A WAX MODEL

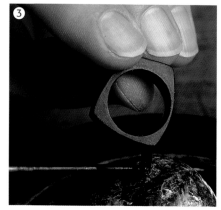

1 Hard wax can be cut with a bandsaw. Drill finger holes with a large spade bit.

2 Use coarse files to rough out a form, then refine it with fine files and sandpaper.

3 Mount the ring model onto a rubber sprue base.

to its unique possibilities, and save the best examples for later. In the meantime, use your experiments to test your skills at spruing, investing and casting, so when the time is right, you'll be confident of your abilities.

It's also worth noting that there are companies in the business of casting other people's models, so you don't necessarily need to master the process to add casting to your repertoire of jewelry making options. Of course, you will pay for this service, and lose the start-to-finish control, but commercial casters offer a useful way to get started; look for addresses in the appendix.

Model making is a personal and vast territory, and stretches far beyond the scope of this book. I do want to point out, however, that whatever you put into the model will come through. If the model has scratches, they'll be there in the casting. If the model seems awkward or out of balance, the same will be true of the casting, darn it. Of course, you want to see the piece in metal, so it's tempting to move on to the next step quickly, but remind yourself that a correction or refinement that takes just a few minutes in wax might take ten times as long in metal. Refine soft waxes with a warm needle drifted lightly across the surface of the form. Carving waxes can be smoothed by rubbing them with a piece of fabric or Scotch-Brite.

SPRUING

Guidelines for Sprues

- Attach sprues to the thickest section of the casting.
- Keep sprues as short as possible.
- Attach sprues where they will be easiest to remove.
- Use a sprue for each major section of a piece.

Xueli Shi, ring. Sterling.

- No part of the casting can be "upstream" from the point of attachment.
- Avoid sharp turns, abrupt edges and narrow joints.

The sprue is the channel that feeds molten metal into the mold cavity. If it is poorly arranged, the mold won't fill, so its importance cannot be overstated.

Although the sprue is important, it is not necessarily complicated. Just remember that at the moment the metal enters the mold, it is fluid, so you can use what you know about fluids to inform your process. For instance, liquids do not flow uphill, so arrange the sprues in such a way that the entire piece is downstream from the point of entry. Keep the sprue walls smooth, so the metal is not stirred up as it enters but, rather, flows as efficiently as possible.

Sprues can be made of any kind of wax, but I recommend using the soft wax made just for this purpose. It's called, guess what, *sprue wax*, and comes in round rods of several hefty sizes. I suggest something around 8 gauge, particularly since this wax is easily rolled out between the palms to make it thinner when needed. One advantage of using a soft wax is that the sprues can be bent after attachment for subtle corrections.

Determine the ideal location for the sprue and hold it in position to select the correct angle. Warm the needle tool, then touch it to the bottom of the sprue rod and press the rod gently onto the model. Hold the pieces steady for a few seconds and the job is done. The same technique is used to secure the other end of the sprue to the base.

It's important that the sprue flare slightly where it attaches to both the piece and the base. To achieve this, warm a needle, point it at the junction area, and touch a piece of wax to the needle about a half inch from its tip. The wax will melt onto the needle, forming a droplet that will slide to the end of the tool and drop onto the sprue.

Stacey Lane, ring. Sterling, 14K, peridot. *Photo by Gregory Staley.*

Specific Gravity of Popular Jewelry Metals	
Brass	8.7
Bronze	8.8
18K yellow gold	15.5
14K yellow gold	13.4
10K yellow gold	11.6
Fine silver	10.6
Sterling	10.4

DETERMINING THE AMOUNT OF METAL

It's always possible to guess at the amount of metal you'll need for a casting, but there are a couple of more scientific solutions. The first requires an accurate balance scale. Weigh the sprued model and multiply that figure by the specific gravity of the metal being cast. The total will be the exact weight of the metal object and sprues. Add at least half that again to allow for the *button*—the excess lump that will supply the casting with additional metal as it cools.

If you don't have a balance, fill a small jar with water and stick a piece of tape vertically along the side. Mark the water level on the jar, then attach the model to a wire and plunge it into the water, making another mark to note the rise of the water level. Remove the model and drop metal scraps into the jar until the level returns to the high mark, then add a little more to allow for the sprue and button.

INVESTING

The piece can be invested as soon as it is mounted onto the sprue base, a hard rubber disk with a lip that secures it to a flask. Most sprue bases have a hemispherical

Sprued models. It is typical to cast several models in the same flask. Allow at least ¼" between pieces, and be sure each model is properly sprued. Notice the use of a secondary sprue on the piece to the right.

Nancy E. Fleming, *Waiting for Guinevere* brooch. Cast sterling twig, brass, 14K, boulder opal. 3 x 1¼".

lump in the center upon which to mount the models. Several models can be cast in the same flask as long as you can follow these rules:

Investing Guidelines

- Each piece must have sufficient sprue to supply all the metal it needs.
- The models must have a quarter-inch clearance from each other, and a half-inch clearance from the sides and top of the flask.
- The sprues should all attach on the upper half of the sprue base dome.

Investing is a messy process and a dangerous one for the unprotected. Work on a cleanable surface like plastic, and expect to spend a little time cleaning up at the end of the process. You'll be using relatively harsh chemicals, so it's wise to wear rubber gloves. Investment powder contains plaster and silicon, which are harmful to the lungs. Work with adequate ventilation, minimize dust, and wear an appropriate respirator. Lung damage doesn't necessarily show up the first day you fail to observe safety rules, but ignoring these

rules can lead to serious respiratory difficulties over time.

Investment powder is hydroscopic, which means it is eager to combine with moisture. For this reason, keep it tightly sealed and be careful not to spill any water into the container. To prepare investment for casting, start by filling a rubber bowl with clean water equivalent to at least two-thirds of the flask volume. If the tap water in your area is loaded with minerals, use bottled water.

Note the time on a clock and start to sprinkle investment powder into the water, where it will sink. Continue sifting, keeping an eye out for lumps and discarding any you find. The powder will eventually start to show, just beneath the surface, as the mixture becomes saturated. Add a little more investment until the powder forms an island in the center of the bowl, then it's time to mix. I use my fingers, but some people feel a spatula is the proper tool. Try both to see which works better for you. I like the feel of the stuff, and use the stirring action to look for any lumps that I might have missed before. Either way, be sure to mix the investment and water with slow strokes to avoid whipping air into the mixture.

Bubbles in the investment tend to attach themselves to the model like bubbles in soda collect on a straw. After burnout, when the wax is gone, these bubbles become voids connected to the area that was the model, and it all looks the same to the molten metal as it comes barreling into the mold. The metal will fill both the model and the spherical bubble spaces, creating "warts" on the surface of the casting. Of course, a few of these on an exposed area can be removed easily, but imagine a thousand nestled into every cranny of your laboriously carved design! You can see

J. Fred Woell, *Great Moments on the Prairie* brooch. Brass, steel, cast sterling. 2¼ x 2¾".

why it's important to get the bubbles out of the investment.

One way to do this is to tap the sides of the rubber bowl to vibrate the bubbles to the surface. A better way is to use a vacuum pump to literally pull air from within the mix. This machine works in conjunction with a bell jar and creates a vacuum by sucking air from within the enclosed space. If the bowl of investment is within that space, air trapped in the investment is pulled out as well.

Once the mixture is creamy—3 to 4 minutes should have elapsed since the start of the process—set the bowl on a rubber pad and cover it with the bell jar. Start the pump and direct the action to the jar, pressing down on it if needed to make a seal. In about a minute you'll see the investment swell up and froth as air is pulled out. Continue until the frothing starts to spit droplets of investment on the inside of the bell jar—about a minute and a half.

Remove the jar and pour the investment into the flask. As you do this, hold on to the base and pour the investment down the side of the flask to avoid having its weight fall directly onto the model. Fill the flask to within a half inch of the top, set it onto the rubber pad and cover it with the bell jar. Repeat the vacuuming process as before to remove any last bubbles. At the end of this process the time elapsed since the powder first touched the water should be about 9 minutes.

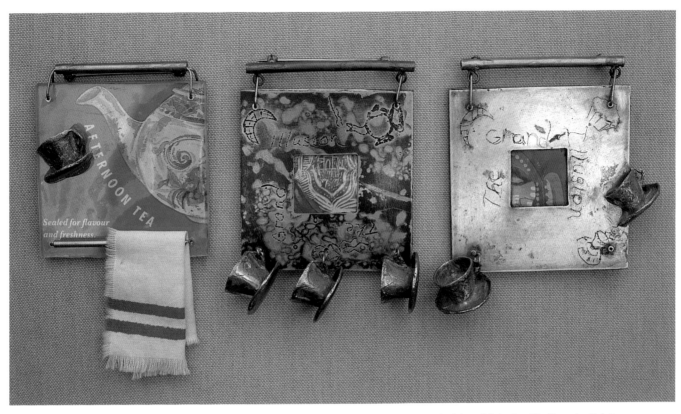

Kimberly Navratil-Pope, *Grand Illusion Series* three brooches. Sterling, bronze, copper, paper, plexiglass, fabric. 2 x 2". *Photo by Rick Pope.*

INVESTMENT CASTING

1 Sprinkle investment powder into water.

2 After a minute in a vacuum, the investment is free of bubbles.

3 Pour the creamy investment down the side of the flask.

(Continued on page 114.)

This is just what you want. Pace yourself so the entire investing process takes between 9 and 10 minutes. If you go too fast, the investment will separate before it hardens; too slow and the investment will set up before you are ready.

When the investing process is complete, set the flask aside for half an hour to harden. This is the start of the curing process, and involves an exothermic (heat-creating) reaction, so you'll notice the flask getting warm.

The rubber base can be pulled off as soon as the investment becomes hard, but a full 2 hours is recommended before beginning the burnout process. Because all filled flasks look the same, mark the flask with relevant information: name, metal to be cast, amount needed, etc. Use chalk to write on the side of the flask or scratch the information into the top of the mold as soon as it is hard enough.

BURNOUT

Purposes of Burnout

- Cure the investment.
- Remove the wax model.
- Heat the mold in preparation for casting.

The ideal drying time for a flask is overnight, but anything from 2 to 24 hours is acceptable. If the flask is not allowed to dry thoroughly, moisture trapped in the investment will turn to steam in the kiln, which will break open the mold as it expands. If a flask waits several days between investing and casting, it can become so dry that the investment is slightly weakened. To avoid this, wrap the piece lightly in plastic, or hold the dried flask under water for a few seconds to renew it before putting it in the kiln.

Take a moment to plan ahead for the next step while it's still possible to hold the flask in your hands—later it will be very hot. Set the flask temporarily into the casting machine, using a metal strip called a *cradle*, if necessary, to lift the mouth of the flask into alignment with the crucible spout. Most casting machines have a mechanism to balance the arm; this does not need to be set precisely, but move the weight outward from the center for a large flask and inward for a small one.

During burnout, the flask must reach a temperature of 1250°F (670°C) to completely evacuate the mold. This can be done in a small kiln and should take about two hours. Set the flask, opening down, onto a wire mesh or propped up on a bit of brick to allow a space for the melting wax to exit.

Turn on the kiln and allow it to heat up, going slowly for the first half hour or so while the wax melts away. During this phase you'll notice a strong odor and some smoke in the room; both should be vented outdoors. If you don't have a so-

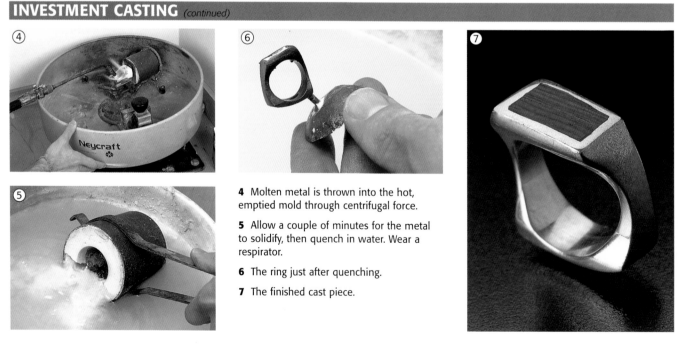

INVESTMENT CASTING *(continued)*

④

⑤

⑥

⑦

4 Molten metal is thrown into the hot, emptied mold through centrifugal force.

5 Allow a couple of minutes for the metal to solidify, then quench in water. Wear a respirator.

6 The ring just after quenching.

7 The finished cast piece.

Nancy Moyer, *Endowment Series* brooch. Sterling, amethyst. 3½ x 3".

phisticated ventilation system, set a small fan on one side of the room and open a window on the other. Happily, the wax-burning stage is soon over.

Continue to heat the flask to 1250°F. Some kilns are outfitted with a pyrometer or temperature dial, but you can also gauge the temperature with potters' pyrometric cones. If you don't have any of these devices, check the flask every half hour; you'll be looking for the time when the sooty deposit around the mouth of the flask burns away, either disappearing completely or leaving only a pale stain. At that point, you can turn off the kiln and begin the final (and in some ways most dramatic) stage of the process.

THROWING THE CASTING

Wind the arm of the casting machine three complete turns and lock it in place with its holding pin. Wear gloves and use tongs to move the flask directly into the prepared machine. The flask should be between 800-1000°F (425-540°C) for casting most metals; the time it takes to work efficiently toward the next step seems to allow just the right amount of cooling.

Set your metal into the crucible and heat it with a strong *reducing* (fuel-rich) flame—one that looks bushy and red-orange. Add a pinch of flux to the metal midway through the melt. When the molten mass starts to spin and quiver, get a firm grip on the end of the casting arm and pull it slightly to release the holding mechanism. Continue to heat the metal, check it one

more time to be sure it's fluid, then simultaneously lift the torch and release the arm. The machine will spin forcefully, casting the metal into the mold with sufficient force to inject it into every detail. Turn off the torch and allow the casting machine to come to a natural stop; this may take a couple of minutes.

Lift the flask out with tongs and examine the button, the lump of extra metal that should now fill the hemispherical cavity that was the mouth of the mold. If there's nothing there, check the crucible to be sure the metal didn't get stuck; it's rare, but it happens. If there is no button and no metal in the crucible, check to see if the metal crashed through the mold and came out the back side; again, rare but possible. What you'll probably find is a comfortably large button that half-way fills the hemispheri-

J. Fred Woell, *Home on the Range* belt buckle. Sterling, arrowhead. 2⅛ x 2½".

cal gate, perhaps colored by a little glassy green flux, which is last to slide out of the crucible.

Hold the flask firmly in tongs and quench it in a bucket of water, which will cause a dramatic, sputtering cloud of steam to arise. This steam is laced with silicon, and is probably the most dangerous vapor in the studio, so wear a respirator and even then, stand back. The hot investment will crack away from the mold and the casting, partially revealing your work. Use a butter knife and toothbrush to clean the flask and the casting, allowing the spent investment to fall back into the bucket. To dispose of used investment, pour off the extra water, allow the sludge to dry for a day or so, and throw it out as solid waste.

Of course, you'll want to examine the casting to see how you did, so take a minute to be analytical. One advantage of casting is its technical nature: Nothing happens without a reason, and if you know the reason, you can fix the mistake.

Observation: "Warts"
SOLUTION:

- Work harder to remove bubbles from the investment.
- Mix the investment thicker.

Observation: "Welts" or "trails"
SOLUTION:

- These are caused by water separating from the mix before it hardens; slow down so you use the whole 9 minutes to invest.

Observation: Partial casting
SOLUTION:

- Not enough metal.
- Melt wasn't hot enough.
- Sprues were too thin.

Observation: Porosity (tiny dots)
SOLUTION:

- The metal was overheated.
- The sprues were not attached to the thickest section. This is what occurs when an area is starved for additional metal as it cools.

OTHER MODELS

Any material that burns out completely can be used to make models. In our plastic-infused culture, this opens the door to all sorts of delightful possibilities. As you can see from the examples shown throughout this book, plastic model parts, containers and industrial components can all become jewelry when manipulated by a creative mind. And that's the trick: to enhance the symbolism and whimsy through reuse, rather than to simply appropriate someone else's skill at carving.

Another fine model material is Styrofoam, particularly the dense variety made for insulation. You can also roll out a slab of clay and press shapes into it, then brush the indented form with wax melted in a double boiler. Plastic or pre-made wax objects can also be embedded here; the various colors and shapes will all blend in the casting process. Burning Styrofoam and plastic create noxious fumes, so effective ventilation is critical.

Appendices

Tim McCreight, fibula. Sterling. 4" long. *Photo by Robert Diamante.*

Sara Shepherd, *Therapy II* brooch. Sterling, 18K. 2 x 1 x 1". *Photo by Douglas Yaple.*

Appendix A

What Do You Need to Know About Metal?

For most people, the pleasure of making jewelry comes from time spent at a workbench, actively driving tools to cut, bend and assemble a piece. A fundamental understanding of the material you'll be using—metal—will increase that pleasure, as well as your rate of success as a jeweler.

Metallurgy

Metals are made of crystals that arrange themselves in a regular pattern called a lattice. This has a lot to do with the physical properties of a metal. Metals with the same crystal lattice will probably have similar density, malleability, conductivity, and so on.

Crystals, also called grains, are clusters of molecules gathered into units whose structure determines the ability of metal to bend, conduct heat and reflect light. All of these attributes are important to jewelers. When grains are small, a sample will be harder to bend, more likely to break, tougher, and a better conductor of electricity. Large crystals make a metal more responsive to patinas and more malleable, except when the grains are very large, which causes the metal to become tough again.

The usual way grains become small is through hammering or rolling. Do this enough and a sample of metal will eventually break, as the grain boundaries become too small to hold the piece intact. This process is called *work hardening*. Its opposite, *annealing*, uses heat to recrystallize the internal structure, building large grains from small ones. All of this goes on at a microscopic level. Annealing temperatures vary with each metal and alloy, but as a rule of thumb they are about two-thirds the melting temperature of a pure metal. Annealing can be done as often as necessary.

Metals and Alloys

This is a huge topic, even taken quickly, so we'll confine ourselves to a discussion of the metals used by beginning jewelry makers: copper, brass, silver and gold. Three of these are pure metals, while one, brass, is a mixture, or *alloy*, of two metals. Pure metals, also called *fine*, are often too soft for wearable jewelry, so they are alloyed as well.

PRECIOUS METALS

Fine gold is given the arbitrary designation "24," so we can say that of 24 parts, all 24 are gold. In the case of 18-karat gold, 18 of the 24 parts are gold, with the balance being something of lesser value. If you write this as a fraction, $18/24$, and reduce it, you'll see that 18-karat gold is three-fourths gold and one-fourth something else. Generally speaking, alloys of 18K and purer are called *high-karat* golds.

The additive ingredients in alloys are used to affect the color, strength, ductility and value of the resulting alloy. In the case of yellow gold, equal parts of silver and copper are added. Rose gold (also called pink gold) is made by increasing the proportion of copper, and green gold is made by increasing the percentage of silver. Note that in all colors the proportion of gold remains the same.

The most popular gold alloy for jewelry in the United States is 14 karat, which is also written as .585, or 58.5 percent gold. The balance can be anything, but it is usually some combination of silver and copper, except in the case of white gold, where platinum, palladium and nickel are used to change the color.

Pure silver is occasionally used in jewelry components, particularly when malleability is an asset. This is the case with bezels, which need to be safely pressed down against a gem. For most applications, however, fine silver is too soft, so a small amount of copper is added for strength. Hundreds of years ago, it was determined that the addition of 7 1/2 percent copper created a metal strong enough to stand up to use while retaining the warm shine of silver. This alloy came to be called *sterling*, and it is far and away the most commonly used silver alloy for jewelry. A slightly baser alloy that contains 10 percent copper was used for hundreds of years in coins, and is therefore called coin silver. It is rarely seen today, except in older pieces. Coins minted in the United States have not contained silver since 1966.

BASE METALS

Copper is used in jewelry for its color, which is orange when polished, brown with normal wear, and green or blue after exposure to certain atmospheres. It is inexpensive, malleable, resilient and attractive, but its one shortcoming is the fact that copper not only discolors when worn, but discolors the wearer as well—typically by turning skin green. This is because of copper's eagerness to combine with almost any element that passes by, from oxygen to ammonia. Despite these shortcomings, jewelers value copper for its colors; it is usually patinated and sealed to protect the metal from further corrosion. Because its malleability is similar to sterling, it also makes an excellent practice material. It is slightly more difficult to solder because of its tendency to oxidize, but this means that a person who has mastered soldering by experimenting with copper will find the transition to sterling especially easy.

Another of copper's virtues is its affinity with other metals. As described above, copper is used to strengthen gold and silver. When

James MaloneBeach, *Northwoods Grandmother* medallion. Sterling, patchwork quilt, rose petal beads, Ohio Blue Tip match. 5½ x 2⅜".

Deborah Krupenia, *Swivel Rings: Four Variations.* Colored golds, fine silver, Japanese copper alloys, sterling, fumed bronze. *Photo by Dean Powell.*

alloyed with the low-melting gray metal called zinc, copper pulls a magician's trick to yield a metal—brass—that is yellow and has a higher melting point than either of its constituents.

By definition, brass is a mixture of copper and zinc, but the proportions can vary and will yield a wide range of results. The most common mix, called *yellow brass,* or *CDA 260,* is 30 percent zinc and 70 percent copper. As the proportion of copper increases, the color becomes more golden and the metal more malleable. An alloy of about 88 percent copper called NuGold is widely used in jewelry making, as are other low-zinc brasses.

Nickel silver, also called German silver, deserves mention not only because it is useful in jewelry, but because its name is so misleading. It contains no silver, and does not come from Germany. It is an alloy of copper, zinc and the element nickel. To see what it looks like, search your pocket change for a 5¢ piece. I prefer to call this alloy "white brass" because it is so similar to yellow brass in cost, malleability, and the way it solders.

So is that it for alloys? Is that all you need to know? Well, not exactly. The photo captions throughout this book refer to higher karats of gold, to steel, to bronze and to Japanese alloys (which typically are copper-based). These alloys offer a fascinating wealth of opportunity for jewelers, and you will begin to use them as your metalsmithing skills develop.

Appendix B
Health & Safety

Every time we touch tools, whether we're holding a paring knife in the kitchen or a scribe in the jewelry studio, we open ourselves to some risk. It would be silly to let these small risks prevent us from, say, peeling an apple, but just as silly to ignore them completely.

This holds true for the kinds of environmental hazards involved in jewelry making, as well.

Common Sense

More than any device, more than any instruction, more than any expensive system, the best tool for long and safe studio work is already within you: your common sense. To refresh your memory, here are a few things you probably already know, but may need to be reminded of:

- If you are unfamiliar with a tool, ask for help.
- Listen to your body. If you feel dizzy, congested, overheated or drowsy, it might be the result of a chemical reaction. Stop what you are doing until you know what's happening.
- Accidents happen ... well ... by accident. Because you can't see them coming, you always have to be prepared. Wear goggles, gloves, an apron, and similar protective clothing any time they might be needed.

Jung-Hoo Kim, *Coexistence* brooch. Sterling, fossilized ivory, sugelite, 24K foil. 3 x 2¼".

Tom Herman,
pin. 18K,
petrified
palmwood,
turquoise,
citrine.
2¼ x 2¾".
*Photo by
George Post.*

■ Anticipate the results of every action. What happens if the drill bit breaks? The hammer head loosens? The buffing machine snags? Plan ahead to prevent problems before they occur.

Respirators

There is a difference between a dust mask and a respirator. The first blocks air from coming into the body, like holding a handkerchief over your mouth. It's better than no protection, but inhibits breathing and only catches relatively large particles. The fibrous paper masks available from hardware stores have the second disadvantage of making only a loose fit, which allows contaminated air in around the edges.

A respirator is fitted with disposable cartridges that actively catch specific particles or fumes. These are much better than paper dust masks, but only as good as your maintenance allows them to be. Keep cartridges sealed when not in use; they are always activated and can fill up simply sitting open on a shelf. Use the correct cartridge for the dust or vapor to which you are exposed, and replace the cartridges when they are depleted.

A proper respirator costs around $25; you *must* have one.

Goggles

These are available in so many styles and prices that there is simply no reason not to own a pair—or several pairs. If you forget to take yours with you when you go from one part of the studio to another, buy a 6-pack and leave them around the studio so they are always within reach. I recommend a fully enclosed design that fits snugly. It will best protect your eyes from debris coming in from the side.

Food and Drink

Eat, drink and be merry, but not in the studio. Airborne particles and fumes will fall into snacks and cups on the bench and then be ingested. Dust that gathers on your hands will come off on your sandwich or cigarette, and from there it's a quick trip into your mouth.

Alan Burton Thompson, *Shadow Box* brooch. Sterling, brass, copper, Bakelite, gold leaf, paper. 4¾ x 2¼".

Special Cases

In writing this book, I've tried to avoid processes that involve dangerous chemicals. However, there are a few procedures where this is not possible. Please note the potential dangers in these activities:

SOLDERING

- The fumes of borax-based flux make some people dizzy.
- At one time, solders contained a harmful metal called cadmium. Accordingly, you should avoid using low-melting solders unless you know they were recently manufactured.

FINISHING

- Some patina solutions are harmful to the skin and if ingested. Wear rubber gloves and a respirator for gun bluing, green patina, and ammonia.

CASTING

- Do not overheat brass; it will release noxious zinc fumes. To avoid this risk, use a brass alloy specifically sold for casting.
- Wear a respirator when handling investment, both in the initial mixing stage and when the flask is quenched.

Appendix C
Pouring an Ingot

Most jewelers purchase metal ready to use, but it's possible to make your own sheet and wire as shown here. Besides the pleasure and convenience of the process, it's useful to know how to recycle scraps.

1 Ingot molds are available commercially and can also be improvised from sheets of steel and bent steel rod. Either way, molds should be massive to hold heat.

2 Prepare the mold by coating it with Vaseline, oil or, as shown, soot from a candle or acetylene torch. This will create a reducing (oxygen-free) atmosphere inside the mold.

3 Cinch the mold with a C-clamp and set it in a container that will safely catch spills, such as a cast-iron skillet.

4 Warm the ingot mold with a large torch until it is hot enough to feel uncomfortable when you hold your hand a couple of inches above the mold.

5 Heat scrap metal in an open pouring crucible, a ladle made of high-fire ceramic. Before the first use of this tool, heat it to red and sprinkle in powdered borax to coat the chamber. Use a pinch of borax with each melt, also, to protect the metal from oxidation.

6 As the metal becomes fluid, swirl the crucible to ensure that there are no solid areas in the melt. Tilt the ladle so the molten mass is poised on the lip, just above the mold. Pour

POURING AN INGOT

1 Coat the ingot mold with soot; this will create a reducing (purifying) environment.

2 Melt metal in a pouring crucible, adding borax at least once as the metal is heated.

3 Warm the mold and pour the molten mass into it with a smooth, even gesture.

(Continued on page 126.)

Brent Williams, pin. Sterling, postage stamp. 1 x 1½".

through the flame with a steady motion. Don't toss the metal, and don't dribble it.

7 The mold can be opened almost immediately, but it will still be very hot, so use tools to unscrew the clamp and retrieve the ingot. If the pour was interrupted, or if you missed the crucible, simply reset the mold and start over. It's not unusual to take a couple of tries to get it right.

The process for making a wire ingot is identical, except for the shape of the mold. To improvise a wire mold, drill a hole into a fire brick, then use a knife to cut a funnel-shaped opening at the top. The resulting rod will have an irregular surface, but it can be easily filed to make a useful blank from which wire can be rolled or drawn.

POURING AN INGOT (continued)

4 The finished ingot.

5 Pouring into a wire mold.

6 Finished wire ingots. These can be rolled or forged to make wire.

Appendix D

Tool Making: Hardening & Tempering Steel

Follow these instructions to make custom tools—such as the stamp shown below—that will last for many years. Use tool steel, a specific alloy that contains from $1/2$ to $1\,1/2$ percent carbon. This can be purchased from suppliers (ask for O1 or 1075 oil-hardening steel), or recycled from old tools.

1 To anneal (or "unharden") old tools, heat the steel to a bright red and allow it to cool as slowly as possible. This can be accomplished by burying the steel in a bucket of sand or ashes, or by covering it with a firebrick. When using newly purchased steel, this step is not necessary.

2 Cut a length of steel that feels comfortable in your hand, usually between 3" and 5". File both ends to make them flat and perpendicular to the shank.

3 File a taper on the working end to allow easy viewing of the stamp as it addresses the metal. The angle of the taper will obvi-

MAKING A STAMPING PUNCH

1 Square off both ends of a 4" piece of tool steel rod.

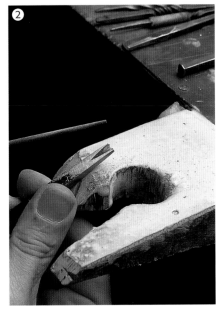

2 Create the intended shape in the end of the rod with a saw and files.

3-4 Refine the shape. The mark can be tested by pressing the tool into clay.

(Continued on page 128.)

ously depend on the shape of the shank compared to the impression being created.

4 Use files, saws, burs and sandpaper to make the tool even, smooth and precise. Touch the tool lightly into clay to test the impression it will create.

5 Use a file to round the top of the tool where the hammer will strike it. This will improve the force of impact and minimize the deflection caused by an angled blow.

6 Grasp the tool in vise grip pliers and heat the lower third to a bright red-orange. The correct temperature can be confirmed by touching the glowing tool to a magnet; at the correct temperature the steel is nonmagnetic.

7 Instantly quench the tool in a can of motor oil, stirring it slowly to cool the steel. Allow it to stay immersed for about a minute, then withdraw it and wipe off the oil.

8 Test the hardening step by sliding a file along the tip of the tool. If hardening was successful, the file will slide across the tool without gripping, making a high-pitched, glassy sound. Repeat steps 6 and 7, if necessary.

9 Sand the tool to remove the gray scale (black oxide) formed in the last step. The next process requires the ability to see the steel change colors, which will be easier on freshly sanded material.

10 Using a small flame, hold the torch stationary about midway along the tool. A band of color will bloom beneath the flame and move toward the tip. Allow the leading edge (straw yellow color) to just reach the tip, then quench instantly—in either oil or water—to avoid heating the tool beyond this point.

11 Strike the tool a dozen times on a piece of scrap metal and examine the imprint it leaves. If the last blow is the same as the first, reach around and pat yourself on the back. You've made a tool!

MAKING A STAMPING PUNCH *(continued)*

5-6 Heat the lower half of the tool to a bright red ... and quench it in oil.

7-8 Sand off the black oxide and heat the steel to a straw yellow color. Quench it instantly. Test the tool by striking it on a piece of scrap metal.

Appendix E
Tool List

BASIC HAND TOOLS

saw frame
pliers
    —chain-nose
    —round-nose
    —flat-nose
    —ring-forming
wire snips
shears
metric ruler
dividers
scribe
tweezers
ring mandrel
drill bits
bezel mandrel
bezel pusher
files
    —hand
    —needle
    —escapement
    —specialty (wax)
hammers
    —rivet
    —planishing
    —ball peen (machinists)
    —forging
    —chasing
mallet (plastic, wood or
    rawhide)

SECONDARY TOOLS

compass
sanding stick
small square
spring gauge or calipers
loupe
pin vise
ring clamp
tube cutting jig
Optivisor
respirator
burnisher
small vise
burs
setting burs
templates

SOLDERING EQUIPMENT

torch
extra torch tips
soldering tweezers
crosslock tweezers
copper tongs
soldering block/fire brick
striker
pickle pot

STUDIO EQUIPMENT

large vise
anvil
dapping block and punches
drawplate and draw tongs
rolling mill
flexible shaft machine
buffing machine
casting machine
burnout kiln
35 mm camera

James MaloneBeach, *Alabama Bugs, Series #1.*
Pebble, millipede, copper. 4³/₄ x 1¹/₂".

Appendix F
Tables & Charts

To convert Centigrade to Fahrenheit:
—Multiply degrees C by 9.
—Divide by 5.
—Add 32.

To convert Fahrenheit to Centigrade:
—Subtract 32 from degrees F.
—Multiply by 5.
—Divide by 9.

°C	°F	°C	°F	°F	°C	°F	°C
0	32	650	1202	32	0	1300	704
50	122	675	1247	100	38	1350	732
75	167	700	1292	150	66	1400	760
100	212	725	1337	200	93	1450	788
125	257	750	1382	250	121	1500	816
150	302	775	1427	300	149	1550	843
175	347	800	1472	350	177	1600	871
200	392	825	1517	400	204	1650	899
225	437	850	1562	450	232	1700	927
250	482	875	1607	500	260	1750	954
275	527	900	1652	550	288	1800	982
300	572	925	1697	600	316	1850	1010
325	617	950	1742	650	343	1900	1038
350	662	975	1787	700	371	1950	1066
375	707	1000	1832	750	399	2000	1093
400	752	1025	1877	800	427	2050	1121
425	797	1050	1922	850	454	2100	1149
450	842	1075	1967	900	482	2150	1177
475	887	1100	2012	950	510	2200	1204
500	932	1125	2057	1000	538	2250	1232
525	977	1150	2102	1050	566	2300	1260
550	1022	1175	2147	1100	593	2350	1288
575	1067	1200	2192	1150	621	2400	1316
600	1112	1225	2237	1200	649	2450	1343
625	1157	1250	2282	1250	677	2500	1371

symbol		Au	Ag	Cu	Zn	other	melting point °C	melting point °F	specific gravity
Al	Aluminum					100 Al	660	1220	2.7
Sb	Antimony					100 Sb	631	1168	6.6
Bi	Bismuth					100 Bi	271	520	9.8
260	Brass, cartridge			70	30		954	1749	8.5
226	Jewelers Bronze			88	12		1030	1886	8.7
220	Red Brass			90	10		1044	1910	8.8
511	Bronze			96		4 Sn	1060	1945	8.8
Cd	Cadmium					100 Cd	321	610	8.7
Cr	Chromium					100 Cr	1890	3434	6.9
Cu	Copper			100			1083	1981	8.9
Au	Gold (fine)	100					1063	1945	19.3
920	22K Yellow	92	4	4			977	1790	17.3
900	22K Coinage	90	10				940	1724	17.2
750	18K Yellow	75	15	10			882	1620	15.5
750	18K Yellow	75	12.5	12.5			904	1660	15.5
750	18K Green	75	25				966	1770	15.6
750	18K Rose	75	5	20			932	1710	15.5
750	18K White	75				25 Pd	904	1660	15.7
580	14K Yellow	58	25	17			802	1476	13.4
580	14K Green	58	35	7			835	1534	13.6
580	14K Rose	58	10	32			827	1520	13.4
580	14K White	58				42 Pd	927	1700	13.7
420	10K Yellow	42	12	41	5		786	1447	11.6
420	10K Yellow	42	7	48	3		876	1609	11.6
420	10K Green	42	58				804	1480	11.7
420	10K Rose	42	10	48			810	1490	11.6
420	10K White	42				58 Pd	927	1760	11.8
Fe	Iron					100 Fe	1535	2793	7.9
Pb	Lead					100 Pb	327	621	11.3
Mg	Magnesium					100 Mg	651	1204	1.7
	Monel Metals			33		60 Ni, 7 Fe	1360	2480	8.9
Ni	Nickel					100 Ni	1455	2651	8.8
752	Nickel Silver			65	17	18 Ni	1110	2030	8.8
Pd	Palladium					100 Pd	1549	2820	12.2
	Old Pewter					80 Pb, 20 Sn	304	580	9.5
Pt	Platinum					100 Pt	1774	3225	21.4
Ag	Silver (fine)		100				961	1762	10.6
925	Sterling		92.5	7.5			920	1640	10.4
800	Coin Silver		80	20			890	1634	10.3
	Mild Steel					99 Fe, 1 C	1511	2750	7.9
	Stainless Steel					91 Fe, 9 Cr	1371	2500	7.8
Sn	Tin					100 Sn	232	450	7.3
Ti	Titanium					100 Ti	1800	3272	4.5
Zn	Zinc				100		419	786	7.1

ALLOYS

WEIGHT PER SQUARE INCH OF SHEET

mm	inch	B&S	fine silver OUNCES	sterling OUNCES	fine gold DWTS. *	10K DWTS.	14K DWTS.	18K DWTS.	platinum OUNCES
6.54	.2576	2	1.42	1.41	52.5	31.4	35.5	42.3	2.91
5.19	.2043	4	1.12	1.12	41.6	24.9	28.1	33.6	2.31
4.11	.1620	6	.894	.884	33.0	19.8	22.3	26.6	1.83
3.26	.1285	8	.709	.701	26.2	15.7	17.7	21.1	1.45
2.59	.1019	10	.562	.556	20.8	12.4	14.0	16.7	1.15
2.05	.0808	12	.446	.441	16.5	9.85	11.1	13.3	.913
1.63	.0641	14	.354	.350	13.1	7.81	8.82	10.5	.724
1.29	.0508	16	.281	.277	10.4	6.21	7.00	8.35	.574
1.02	.0403	18	.223	.220	8.20	4.91	5.55	6.62	.455
.813	.0320	20	.176	.174	6.51	3.90	4.40	5.25	.361
.643	.0253	22	.140	.138	5.16	3.09	3.49	4.216	.286
.511	.0201	24	.111	.110	4.09	2.45	2.77	3.30	.227
.404	.0154	26	.088	.087	3.24	1.94	2.19	2.62	.180
.330	.0126	28	.070	.069	2.58	1.54	1.74	2.08	.143
.254	.0100	30	.055	.055	2.04	1.22	1.38	1.65	.113

WEIGHT PER FOOT OF WIRE

mm	inch	B&S	fine silver OUNCES	sterling OUNCES	fine gold DWTS. *	10K DWTS.	14K DWTS.	18K DWTS.	platinum OUNCES
6.54	.2576	2	3.45	3.41	128	76.3	86.1	104	7.07
5.19	.2043	4	2.17	2.14	80.1	48.0	54.2	64.6	4.45
4.11	.1620	6	1.36	1.35	50.4	30.2	34.1	40.6	2.80
3.26	.1285	8	.856	.848	31.6	19.0	21.4	25.6	1.76
2.59	.1019	10	.541	.534	20.0	11.9	13.5	16.1	1.11
2.05	.0808	12	.339	.335	12.6	7.50	8.47	10.1	.695
1.63	.0641	14	.214	.211	7.87	4.72	5.33	6.36	.437
1.29	.0508	16	.135	.132	4.96	2.97	3.35	4.00	.275
1.02	.0403	18	.085	.084	3.11	1.87	2.11	2.51	.173
.813	.0320	20	.053	.053	1.96	1.17	1.33	1.58	.109
.643	.0253	22	.034	.033	1.28	.738	.833	.994	.068
.511	.0201	24	.021	.021	.775	.464	.524	.625	.043
.404	.0154	26	.013	.013	.488	.292	.330	.393	.027
.330	.0126	28	.008	.008	.306	.184	.287	.247	.017
.254	.0100	30	.005	.005	.193	.115	.130	.155	.010

* DWTS. = pennyweights

To find the weight of a given object if it were made in a different metal, multiply by the factors shown. For instance, if I have a sterling ring that weighs 6 dwts. (known) and I want to know its weight in 18K yellow gold (query), **6 x 1.48 = 8.8 dwts.** (pennyweights).

Query	Known	Factor
18KY (yellow) Gold	18KW (white)	1.064
	platinum	.723
	brass	1.885
	sterling	1.480
14KY Gold	18KW	.842
	14KW	1.035
	platinum	.609
	brass	1.589
	sterling	1.248
10KY Gold	18 KY	.745
	14 KW	.884
	platinum	.539
	brass	1.406
	sterling	1.104
Platinum	palladium	1.758
	iridium	.953
	10% irid plat	.995
	15% irid plat	.993
	rhodium	1.717
	ruthenium	1.771
	sterling	2.046
Sterling	fine silver	.984
	coin silver	1.004
	18KY	.675
	14KY	.801
	10KY	.905
	platinum	.488
	brass	1.273

RELATIVE SIZES & WEIGHTS

B&S	mm	inches thousandths/fractions		drill size
0	8.5	.325	21/64	
1	7.35	.289	9/32	
2	6.54	.258	1/4	
3	5.83	.229	7/32	1
4	5.19	.204	13/64	6
5	4.62	.182	3/16	15
6	4.11	.162	5/32	20
7	3.67	.144	9/64	27
8	3.26	.129	1/8	30
10	2.59	.102		38
11	2.30	.090	3/32	43
12	2.05	.080	5/64	46
13	1.83	.072		50
14	1.63	.064	1/16	51
15	1.45	.057		52
16	1.29	.050		54
17	1.15	.045	3/64	55
18	1.02	.040		56
19	.912	.036		60
20	.813	.032	1/32	65
21	.724	.029		67
22	.643	.025		70
23	.574	.023		71
24	.511	.020		74
25	.455	.018		75
26	.404	.016	1/64	77
27	.361	.014		78
28	.330	.013		79
29	.279	.011		80
30	.254	.010		

Appendix G
Glossary

Like any other trade, jewelry making has its own vocabulary—one rich with tradition and meaning. Here are some of the words that have special meaning in metalsmithing, along with brief, non-technical definitions.

Abrasives. Coarse particles of natural sands and synthetic materials used to scrape away irregularities on a surface. The most common form is sandpaper, properly called *coated stock*.

Aluminum. A light-weight, silver-colored metal used extensively in commercial applications, but seldom in jewelry making. Aluminum can be welded only with special equipment. In a process called anodizing, aluminum is given a tough porous coating that can be colored with dyes.

Annealing. The process of rendering metal more malleable by heating it to a specific temperature.

Basket setting. Any stone setting characterized by an open grillwork around the lower part of the stone.

Bench pin. A wooden extension of a jeweler's bench against which filing, sawing and forming are done.

Bezel. A wall of metal that surrounds a gemstone and secures it in place.

Bezel pusher. A short piece of brass or steel set into a bulbous handle and used to press a bezel down onto a gemstone.

Box catch. A type of closure in which a springy "tongue" snaps into place in a snugly fitting box to secure a necklace or bracelet.

Brass. An alloy of copper and zinc. Brass is yellow in color, and though harder than either of its constituents, it is appropriately malleable for jewelry making.

Brazing. High-temperature soldering that yields a particularly strong joint.

Bronze. Traditionally, an alloy of copper and tin widely used in casting. The term is often applied to brown-colored brasses.

Brooch. A pin in which the stem is completely hidden when the object is being worn. See Fibula.

Burn out. The stage in the casting process when heat is used to cure the mold and remove the model.

Burnisher. A polished steel or stone tool used to polish metal.

Buffing. The final stage of creating a high polish, in which fine abrasives are rubbed against metal to smooth away minor surface irregularities. Buffing can be done with hand tools or machines.

Carat. A unit of weight, originally determined by a carob seed, used in measuring gemstones. A carat contains 100 points. Not to be confused with "karat."

Chamfer. A beveled edge.

Chasing. A technique in which steel tools (punches) are used to decorate and/or texture a surface.

Copper. A popular and versatile metal. Copper is known for its malleability, low cost and wide range of patinas.

Cradle hinge. A hinge in which the individual knuckles are contained in a trough, or cradle.

Cross peen hammer. Any wedge-shaped hammer face. These are used to push the metal in controlled directions when forging, riveting, raising, and setting stones.

Crown setting. A symmetrical prong setting that looks like a miniature crown.

Cuttlefish. A marine animal whose porous white skeleton is used as a mold in one kind of direct casting.

Dapping block. A steel tool—typically a cube—into which have been cut various sizes of round hemispherical depressions. It is used to form domes. The steel rods with matching domes on the ends are called dapping punches.

Depletion gilding. The process of establishing a layer of pure metal on a piece by leaching out the base metal components of the alloy. In the case of sterling, for example, acid (pickle) is used to remove the copper from the alloy, creating a thin "skin" of fine (pure) silver.

Drawplate. A tool of hardened steel used to reduce wire in size. Drawplates consist of a series of funnel-shaped holes of diminishing size, and can be purchased in many shapes, such as round, half-round, square, and triangular.

Fibula. An ornamental and functional pin in which the mechanical elements (pinstem and catch) are integral to the design. This ancient format was the progenitor of the common safety pin.

Findings. This broad term refers to any element that contributes to the wearability of a piece of jewelry, such as pins, earwires and chains.

Firescale. A "stain" of oxidized copper that penetrates sterling and low-karat gold when the metal is overheated.

Flame types. A flame in which all available fuel is consumed and no excess oxygen remains is called "neutral" or "balanced." A fuel-rich flame is called "reducing" and an oxygen-rich flame is called "oxidizing." The former is bushy and often shows yellow fins; the latter is pale blue and hissing.

Flex shaft. A versatile studio tool consisting of a precision high-speed motor, a foot rheostat and a 3-foot extension that allows manipulation of the handpiece. It is used for drilling, grinding, sanding, carving and polishing.

Flux. A chemical employed during soldering to protect metal against the formation of oxides.

Forging. The process of shaping metal primarily through the use of a hammer. Most nonferrous metals are forged at room temperature, while steel and iron are worked at red heat.

Fusing. The technique of joining metals by melting them together.

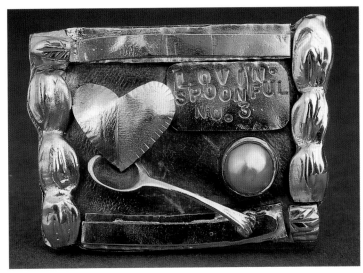

Jenepher Burton, *Loving Spoonful No. 3* brooch. 18K, sterling, pearl. 2¼ x 3".
Photo by Robert Diamante.

Gold. An element long treasured for its ability to shine, resist corrosion, and join. Pure gold is usually alloyed with other metals, typically silver and copper, to create tougher materials of similar characteristics.

Ingot. A massive unit of metal, typically cast as the first step in creating sheet and wire of a more usable size.

Investment. A plaster that contains cristobalite to allow it to remain solid at high temperatures. It is used to make molds in lost wax casting.

Japanese alloys. A general term for alloys widely used in Japan, such as *shibuishi, kuromido* and *shakudo*. These copper-based alloys are especially favored for their ability to take striking and unusual patina colors.

Karat. A proportional unit used to describe the purity of gold alloys. Based on the number 24, gold alloys can be described by the percentage of gold in a sample: 14 karat, for instance, refers to the fraction $14/24$, or 58.5 percent gold. A more scientific description, gaining in popularity and standard in Europe, refers to parts per thousand, for example, .585.

Layout. The process of determining and marking out the elements that will go into a piece of jewelry.

Liver of sulfur. Potassium sulfide, a bad-smelling yellow compound mixed with water to make a solution that will darken copper and sterling.

Lost wax casting. An ancient process through which a wax replica is encased in a mold that is subsequently cured, emptied and refilled with metal. This is a *waste mold* process, which means the mold must be destroyed to recover the casting.

Mallet. A hammer-shaped tool of a material that will not seriously mark metal. Mallets are made of plastic, leather, wood, paper and horn.

Mandrel. A rigid tool, usually steel, against which metal is pressed or hammered to change its shape. Mandrels are usually named after their common use, as in bezel mandrel, ring mandrel and bracelet mandrel.

Model making. The process of creating exact replicas of designs, typically in wax, for reproduction.

Needle files. A large family of narrow files ranging from about 3" to 7" long.

Nickel silver. A tough, corrosion-resistant alloy of copper, zinc and nickel, formerly called "German silver."

Patina. A colored coating on metal. Patinas can happen naturally (as with green copper roofing) or through careful application of chemicals.

Pickle. An acidic solution used to clean metal.

Piercing. Work done with a jeweler's saw, particularly when cutting within a shape.

Pitch. A slightly yielding substance used to support metal during repoussé.

Planishing. The process of smoothing metal with polished hammers.

Prong settings. Stone mountings in which "fingers" of metal secure the gems.

Punches. Hardened steel tools used to decorate, texture and form metal. Punches are roughly the size of short pencils, and can be purchased or made in the studio.

Raising. Forcing metal into volumetric forms through the use of hammers and stakes.

Reactive metals. A family of lightweight metals used in jewelry because of their ability to take and retain oxidation colors through controlled electric current.

Repoussé. An ancient process in which sheet metal is hammered into contours from both the front and the back.

Respirator. A safety device that filters air before it is inhaled by passing it through a chemically active cartridge.

Reticulation. A heat-based process that uses a discrepancy of shrinkage rates to create a rich, somewhat random, texture.

Rifflers. Small files with teeth only on the very tip, often with curved, unusual shapes that make them useful for tight corners. Also called *escapement* files.

Rivets. Mechanical connectors that join elements without the use of heat.

Roll printing. A technique in which a rolling mill is used to imprint textures and patterns under great pressure.

Rolling mill. A piece of equipment consisting of two parallel, hardened steel cylinders mounted in a sturdy frame.

Rubber molds. These reusable molds are used to produce multiple wax models for production lost wax casting.

Sand casting. An ancient and still widely used casting method in which moistened sand is packed against a model to make a mold.

Scoring. Removing metal to create a groove along which metal is bent.

Silver. An element known for its purity, malleability and bright shine. Because pure silver is relatively soft, it is usually alloyed with a small amount of copper to make sterling.

Sinking. The process of pressing metal into a form to create volume.

Sling casting. A low-tech method of developing the centrifugal force needed to create precise castings in some metals.

Solder. An alloy of specific melting point and surface tension used to join metals.

Sprues. The passageways that allow molten metal to enter a mold cavity during casting.

Stakes. Rigid forms, typically of steel, against which metal is hammered to create volumetric shapes in a process called raising.

Stamping. The technique of impressing shapes and textures through hardened tools called punches.

Steel. An alloy of iron and carbon.

Tabs. A cold connection in which fingers or strips of metal are bent over an element to secure it in place.

Thrumming. The use of strings and thongs coated with polishing compound to polish hard-to-reach areas.

Upset. To pound metal down upon itself as, for instance, when making rivets.

Vertigris. A poisonous green compound of copper carbonate. Vertigris is a popular patina on copper and brass.

Work hardening. The characteristic of metals that causes them to toughen through force such as hammering, stretching, drawing, bending, rolling and compressing.

Appendix H
Suppliers

COMPREHENSIVE SUPPLIERS

Allcraft Jewelry Supply
666 Pacific Street
Brooklyn, NY 11217
(800) 645-7124
(212) 840-1860

California Crafts Supply
1201 E. Ball Road #C
Anaheim, CA 92805
(714) 774-4588
(714) 774-4450 fax

William Dixon Company
750 Washington Avenue
Carlstadt, NJ 07072
(800) 847-4188
(201) 939-6700
(201) 939-5067 fax

E. B. Fitler & Company
RD 2, Box 176-B
Milton, DE 19968
(800) 346-2497
(302) 684-1893 fax

Forslev's Jewelry Supply
210 S. Milwaukee Avenue
Wheeling, IL 60090
(847) 520-4120
(847) 520-4437 fax
Forslev@aol.com
http://members.aol.com/forslev/
Catalog.htm

Otto Frei & Jules Borel
126 2nd Street
Oakland, CA 94607
(800) 722-3456
(800) 900-3734 fax
(510) 832-0355
(510) 834-6217 fax
http://www.ofrei.com

Brent Williams, cuff bracelet. Sterling, cast and manipulated model part.

**Paul H. Gesswein
& Company**
255 Hancock Avenue
Bridgeport, CT 06605-0936
(800) 243-4466
(203) 366-5400
(203) 366-3953 fax
gessweinco@aol.com

Grieger's Inc.
2830 E. Foothill Boulevard
Pasadena, CA 91107
(800) 423-4181
(818) 304-7690
(818) 577-4751 fax

C. R. Hill Company
2734 West Eleven Mile Road
Berkley, MI 48072-3078
(800) 521-1221
(313) 543-1555
(313) 543-9104 fax

**Indian Jewelers Supply
Company**
PO Box 1774
Gallup, NM 87305
(800) 545-6540
(505) 722-4451
(505) 722-4172 fax

Rio Grande
7500 Bluewater Road NW
Albuquerque, NM 87121-1962
(800) 545-6566
(display & packaging)
(800) 443-6766
(metal/gems/findings)
(505) 839-3000
(800) 648-3499 fax
http://www.riogrande.com

J.S. Ritter
118 Preble Street
Portland, ME 04101
(800) 962-1468
(207) 772-3822
jsritter@agate.net
http://www.vrmedia.com/jsritter

Swest, Inc.
11090 N. Stemmons Freeway
Dallas, TX 75229
(800) 527-5057
(214) 247-7744
(800) 441-5162 fax

Norman A. Thomas Company
742 N. Old Woodward Avenue
Birmingham, MI 48009
(800) 642-7210
(810) 642-7212
(810) 642-9630 fax

TSI, Inc.
101 Nickerson Street
PO Box 9266
Seattle, WA 98109
(800) 426-9984
(206) 282-3040
(206) 281-8701 fax

REFINERS

David H. Fell & Company
6009 Bandini Boulevard
City of Commerce, CA 90040-2904
(800) 822-1996
(213) 722-9992
(213) 722-6567 fax

Eastern Smelting and Refining
37-39 Bubier Street
Lynn, MA 01901
(800) 343-0914
(617) 599-9000
(617) 598-4880 fax

Hauser & Miller Company
10950 Lin-Valle Drive
St. Louis, MO 63123
(800) 462-7447
(800) 535-3829 fax
(314) 487-1311
(314) 487-0394 fax

Hoover & Strong, Inc.
10700 Trade Road
Richmond, VA 23236-3000
(800) 759-9997
(800) 616-9997 fax
(804) 794-3700
(804) 794-5687
hourgold@ix.netcom.com

Precious Metals West / Fine Gold
608 South Hill Street #407
Los Angeles, CA 90014
(800) 689-4872
(213) 689-1654 fax
Daniel@Westworld.com
http://www.Paleoart.com/pmwest

United Precious Metal Refining
2781 Townline Road
Alden, NY 14004
(800) 999-3463
(716) 683-8334
(800) 533-6657 fax

PRODUCTION CASTING COMPANIES

Alpine Casting Company
3122 Karen Place
Colorado Springs, CO 80907
(800) 365-2278
(719) 442-0711 fax

Art-Tech Casting Company
3894 Scottsville Road
Scottsville, NY 14546
(800) 418-9970
(716) 889-9187
(716) 889-9187 fax

Billanti Casting Company
299 South 11th Street
New Hyde Park, NY 11040
(516) 775-4800
(516) 775-48339

J. A. Henkel Company
14 Maine Street #7
PO Box 661
Brunswick, ME 04011
(207) 729-3599
(207) 729-3723 fax

Larry Paul Casting
740 Sansom Street #410
Philadelphia, PA 19106
(215) 928-1644
(215) 574-1943 fax
Lpaul@aol.com

MISCELLANEOUS

Metalliferous, Inc.
34 West 46th Street
New York, NY 10036-4520
(212) 944-0909
(212) 944-0644 fax

Reactive Metals Studio
PO Box 890
Clarkdale, AZ 86324
(520) 634-3434
(520) 634-6734 fax
reactive@sedona.net
http://www.callasser.com/ezecho/
    rins/rins.html

Microstamp Corporation
2770 E. Walnut Steet
Pasadena, CA 91107
(800) 243-3543
(818) 793-9489
(818) 793-9491 fax

Appendix I
Suggested Reading

Centrifugal or Lost Wax Casting
Murray Bovin
Bovin, Forest Hills, NY
1971, rev. 1977

Classical Loop-in-Loop Chains
J.R. Stark and J.R. Smith
Chapman & Hall, New York, NY
1996

**Coloring, Bronzing and
   Patination of Metals**
Hughes and Rowe
Watson-Guptill, New York, NY
1982

The Complete Metalsmith
Tim McCreight
Davis Publications, Worcester, MA
1982, rev. 1991

Design and Creation of Jewelry
Robert vonNeumann
Chilton Publishers, Radnor, PA
1961, rev. 1972, 1989

Jeweler's Bench Reference
Harold O'Connor
Dunconnor Books, Salida, CO
1977

**Jewelry: Concepts and
   Technology**
Oppi Untracht
Doubleday, New York, NY
1982

Efharis
Alepedis,
ring.
Sterling.
3 x 1 x 1".

**Jewelry: Contemporary Design
   and Technique**
Chuck Evans
Davis Publications, Worcester, MA
1983

Metal Techniques for Craftsmen
Oppi Untracht
Doubleday, New York, NY
1968

Practical Casting
Tim McCreight
Brynmorgen Press,
   Cape Elizabeth, ME
1986

Practical Jewelry Rendering
Tim McCreight
Brynmorgen Press,
   Cape Elizabeth, ME
1995

Professional Goldsmithing
Alan Revere
Revere Academy Books,
   San Francisco, CA
1991

Index

Abrasives 52-56, 58, 134
Acids 39
Adhesives 51
Alcohol lamp 107
Alloy 119-121, 131
Aluminum 134
Annealing 15, 18, 119, 127, 134

Bails 87
Basket setting 82, 134
Bench pin 11, 134
Bezels 70-78, 134
Bezel pusher 74, 134
Binding wire 39
Bobbing 55
Book list 139
Box catch 134
Brass 21-22, 120-121, 134
Brazing 33,134
Bronze 134
Brooches 84-86, 134
Buffing 57-61, 134
Burn out 107, 114-115, 134
Burnishing 56-57
Button 110

Chains 90-97
Chasing 25-26, 134
Chip soldering 36
Clasps 87-90
Coloring (oxidation) 62-66
Collar bezel 75-76
Comparative sizes 133
Comparative weights 131-133
Conversions 130, 132, 133
Copper 120-121, 134
Cross peen 20, 134
Crown setting 79-80, 134
Cuttlefish 103-106, 134

Dapping 17, 134
Depletion gilding 31, 40, 134
Disappearing rivets 48
Diffusion 32-22

Drawing wire 15
Drawplates 15, 135
Drilling 12

Epoxy 51
Etruscan chain 92-95

Files and filing 13-15
Findings 84-91, 135
Firescale 135
Flame types 135
Flex shaft 58
Flux 34-35, 124, 135
Forging 20-21, 135
Fusing 32-22, 135

Gallery wire 70
Gemstones 68-70
Goggles 12, 123
Grades of solder 36
Green patina 66

Hammers 20
Hardening steel 127-128
Health and safety 39, 57, 65, 111, 114,
    116, 122-124
Hinges 99-101
Holding devices 38-39

Ingots 102-103, 125-126, 135
Investment 107, 110-114, 135
Investment soldering 39

Japanese alloys 135
Jump rings 90-91

Kum boo 31

Lamination inlay 31, 40
Layout 9, 10, 135
Liver of sulfur 65-66, 135
Loop-in-loop chain 92-95
Lost wax casting 106-116, 135

Mallets 135
Mandrels 135
Measuring tools 8, 9, 129
Melting points of solder 36
Metallurgy 33,119-121
Modelmaking 107-109, 116, 135
Motors 57-59

Nailhead rivets 49
Needle files 14, 136
Nickel silver 121, 136

Oxide prevention 34-36

Patinas 62-67
Pedestal prong setting 80-83
Pick soldering 37
Pickle 39-41, 136
Piercing 11-12, 79, 136
Pins 84-86
Pitch 136
Planishing 20-21, 136
Plating 40-41
Polishing 57-61
Polishing sticks 56
Prong settings 78-83, 136
Pumice 53
Punches 24-28, 127-128, 136
Puzzle inlay 30

Reactive metals 136
Reducing flame 115, 125
Repoussé 26-28, 136
Respirators 57, 59, 123, 136
Reticulation 29-30, 136
Rifflers 14, 136
Rivets 43-49, 136
Roll printing 21-24, 136
Roman chain 92-95

S-Hook 88
Safety information 39, 57, 65, 111, 114,
    116, 122-124

Sanding sticks 54
Sawing 10-12
Sawblade chart 10
Scoring 17-18, 136
Scratch brush 57
Sealing patinas 66-67
Setting procedures 70-76, 80-83
Silver 120, 131, 136
Solder and soldering 33-41, 136
Solder blocks 32
Solder inlay 24-25
Specific gravity chart 110, 131
Sprues 104, 107, 109-110, 136
Staples 43-44
Stamping 24-25, 136
Steel 127, 131
Sterling 120
Studio equipment 129
Sweat soldering 37

T-Bar clasp 88-90
Tabs 43, 136
Temperature conversion 130
Textures 20-22, 26, 28-30
Threaded connections 50-51
Thrumming 54, 136
Tube rivets 48-49
Tube setting 77
Tweezers 38
Tubemaking 98-99

Vertigris 66, 136

Wax 67, 107-109
White diamond 55
Wire 15-16, 126
Wire soldering 36
Work hardening 119, 139
Woven chains 95-97

Angelina J. Verni, neckpiece (detail). Bronze and rubber.

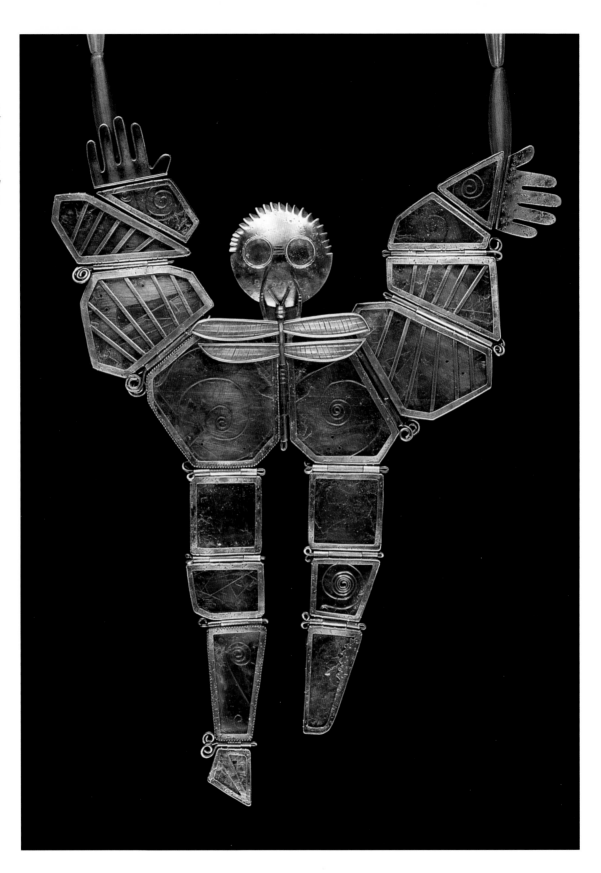

Kiff Slemmons,
*Isinglasses for
Mica Man*
neckpiece.
Sterling, mica.
10 x 8".
*Photo by Rod
Slemmons.*

Acknowledgments

I'd like to thank all the talented designers who have allowed us to include their work here. Bravo, and continued good wishes to each of them. I'd also like to thank Frank Lewis and the staff of *Metalsmith* magazine, who generously opened their photo archives to me. Robert Diamante deserves thanks not only for his rich photographs, but for the genial and gracious support he has contributed throughout. I'd also like to thank Katie Kazan at Hand Books Press, whose precision editing is matched only by her unflappable good humor.

T.M.
Maine, April 1997